THE COMPLETE French Macarons COOKBOOK

THE
COMPLETE
French
Macarons
COOKBOOK

100 Classic and Creative Recipes

NATALIE WONG

PHOTOGRAPHY BY ELYSA WEITALA

ROCKRIDGE
PRESS

For general information on our other products and services or to obtain technical support, please contact our Customer Care Department within the United States at (866) 744-2665, or outside the United States at (510) 253-0500.

Rockridge Press publishes its books in a variety of electronic and print formats. Some content that appears in print may not be available in electronic books, and vice versa.

TRADEMARKS: Rockridge Press and the Rockridge Press logo are trademarks or registered trademarks of Callisto Media Inc. and/or its affiliates, in the United States and other countries, and may not be used without written permission. All other trademarks are the property of their respective owners. Rockridge Press is not associated with any product or vendor mentioned in this book.

Interior and Cover Designer: Linda Snorina
Art Producer: Hannah Dickerson
Editor: Anna Pulley
Production Editor: Andrew Yackira
Production Manager: Riley Hoffman

Photography © 2021 Elysa Weitala, food styling by Victoria Woollard; except for the following: © Marija Vidal, pp. 13, 14, 16 (bottom), 17. All decorative illustrations used under license from Shutterstock.com. Author photo courtesy of Cushman & Wakefield.

Hardcover ISBN: 978-1-68539-603-9
Paperback ISBN: 978-1-63807-042-9
eBook ISBN: 978-1-63807-293-5
R0

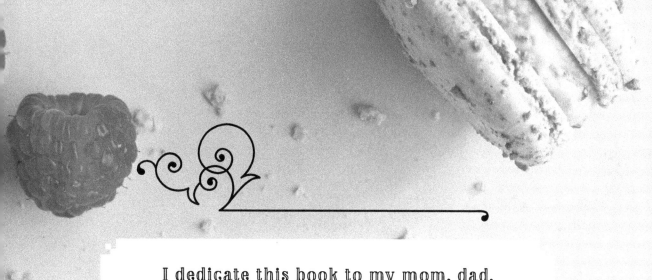

I dedicate this book to my mom, dad, brother, boyfriend, Jevons Jiang, and Auntie Rachel; you guys have been the best supporters from the beginning.

Galaxy Macarons page 116

Contents

Introduction viii

CHAPTER 1: **MACARON FUNDAMENTALS** 1

CHAPTER 2: **THE CLASSICS** 27

CHAPTER 3: **NEW CREATIONS** 65

CHAPTER 4: **HOLIDAYS AND CELEBRATIONS** 107

CHAPTER 5: **VEGAN AND NUT–FREE MACARONS AND FILLINGS** 141

CHAPTER 6: **FILLINGS** 163

Measurement Conversions 199

Resources 200

Index 201

Introduction

When you think of a macaron, what do you envision? I see pâtisseries in Paris, with huge display cases full of macarons in jewellike colors. Taking one out of the beautiful bakery box, you see it has a perfectly even shell-to-filling ratio, with a small ruffle at the bottom. As you bite into it, the slightly crunchy shell gives way to an airy, lightly chewy texture, and the soft, creamy filling bursts with flavor into your mouth.

In recent years, the popularity of macarons has skyrocketed. What suddenly made the rest of the world so crazy for macarons? They're pricier than your average cookie, but once you make them, you will understand why. The rainbow of colors, the endless combinations of flavors, and the beautiful aesthetics of macarons keep people coming back for more. Macarons can also be made into fun and whimsical shapes, making them even harder to resist!

I first saw macarons pop up on Instagram in 2012, and I was intrigued by their dainty size, beautiful colors, and countless flavors. I decided to peruse a French bakery in my hometown, which left me utterly disappointed. They did not make the macarons in rainbow colors; they were all the natural color of off-white and brown. Their flavors were either too sweet or too muted and unrecognizable, and the macarons were crunchy, not soft.

Determined to get my hands on the kinds of macarons I'd seen and heard about, I decided to make them myself. The first time I tried making macarons, they turned out flat, like pancakes! But I couldn't just stand by and fail; I had to try again and research what went wrong. Eventually, I made a beautiful batch of macarons that I posted on Instagram, and people were excited! I kept baking them and began posting my tips and tricks online on my blog. Fast-forward almost 10 years, and here I am, still baking macarons, now as a full-fledged career—and with a recently opened bakery of my own.

When I bake macarons, it brings me joy, and when I teach people how to bake, I feel happy to help others discover the delight of macarons. In this book, I will teach you the basics, as well as more advanced techniques and flavors. We will learn the French method of making macarons, which is the simplest style—no boiling sugar or heating egg whites in this process.

I'll provide you with all the necessary knowledge and techniques to create the perfect batch of macarons and savor the enjoyment that comes along with it. In addition, this book includes some whimsical creations like bear-shaped macarons, heart shapes, and fun holiday flavors, as well as vegan and nut-free options. This book will allow you to dive deep into your creativity and come up with endless combinations and designs.

Fruity Cereal Macarons page 66

Pink with Gold Brush Macarons page 114

CHAPTER 1

Macaron Fundamentals

Raspberry Cheesecake Macarons page 90

THE MADDENING SIMPLICITY OF THE MACARON

The first time I saw a macaron, I was dazzled by its beautiful appearance: smooth shell, vibrant color, and creamy, soft filling. I soon learned that although a basic macaron shell recipe is made of five simple ingredients (almond flour, powdered sugar, granulated sugar, salt, and egg whites), it can be difficult to execute properly. Many factors can change a macaron batch's outcome, which we'll cover in this chapter.

Weather Matters

Macarons are temperamental, especially regarding weather. Although extreme weather conditions can cause baked goods, such as meringues or pies, to come out differently, macarons "take the cake" for the most affected. For example, if it's raining, it's not ideal to bake macarons because the shells take longer to dry. If the shells cannot dry, they'll crack when baked. General humidity also affects drying time. To combat this, you may want to get a dehumidifier if you live in a humid or tropical area, to speed the drying process.

Proper Measurements Matter

Baking macarons is a precise science. If ingredient measurements are off even slightly, the results can be affected. This is why it is crucial to weigh ingredients using a digital kitchen scale, so the result is the same every time. For instance, if you add too much almond flour or powdered sugar, the batter will be too dry and lumpy. Likewise, if you add too much egg white, the batter will be too wet and will crack during baking.

Proper Equipment Matters

For the perfect macarons, you'll want to invest in the proper equipment. This includes a silicone spatula to fold the batter, an electric mixer to whip egg whites, a piping bag to make macaron circles the easiest way, aluminum baking sheets, and silicone mats to bake the macarons on. Technically, you could use simpler tools that you already have, such as a zip-top bag instead of a piping bag, but the result may not be as professional or beautiful.

Temperature Matters

The temperature at which you bake macarons is also extremely important; it can literally make or break the process. If the temperature is too low, the macarons will not rise, or they will be wet, sticky, and fragile inside, creating hollow shells. If the temperature is too high, your macarons will brown, turning them an unpleasant color and making them dry and hard. To prevent any mishaps from baking temperature, I recommend placing an oven thermometer in your oven when you bake macarons to ensure your oven temperature is correct.

Almond Flour Matters

Make sure you use good-quality almond flour in your macarons. Some almond flours are more oily or lumpy than others. If the almond flour is too oily, it can create blotchy oil spots on your macarons. If it's too dry, it can cause the macarons to be lumpy, and the batter may not flow. After testing many flours over the years, I recommend Blue Diamond, Kirkland, Nuts.com, or Amoretti almond flour.

EQUIPPING YOUR KITCHEN

It's vital to stock your kitchen with the proper equipment—this will directly affect your success in the macaron world. Reusable equipment such as piping bags and silicone mats will also keep you prepared whenever your creative urge strikes. Following are the key essentials.

Digital Scale

To me, a digital kitchen scale is the pinnacle of baking equipment. You can use it for any baking recipe, not just macarons! Many French pastry books call for measurements in grams (weight). Recipes from other parts of the globe, such as Korea or Japan, are also measured in grams, so a digital scale can help broaden your recipe repertoire. You can purchase a scale for relatively little money at any larger general merchandise store or online. The scale should include several measurements in addition to grams, such as ounces, milliliters, and pounds.

ABOUT THE MEASUREMENTS IN MY RECIPES

I only use weight measurements for dry ingredients, and weight measurements with a volume equivalent for wet ingredients. This ensures the proportions are correct with little to no room for error. For example, when you use a 1-cup (volume) measurement, you may get a different weight every time. Conversely, when you use a digital kitchen scale, the portion size (weight) is consistent. I also use grams, because it's simpler and more precise than ounces. Grams are smaller measurements and easier to multiply if you have to make larger batches. Weighing egg whites in grams is also more precise, because each egg contains a different amount of egg white. Using a kitchen scale may seem a little daunting at first, but you'll thank me later! The great variabilities in volume measurements are easily thwarted by using a kitchen scale, especially on a notoriously challenging recipe like macarons.

Mixing Bowls

As a baker, you'll want to have a variety of mixing bowls. Invest in nesting mixing bowls, which save room in the kitchen. For sifting almond flour or powdered sugar or making meringue and buttercream, I prefer to use a small- to medium-size bowl, because the batter doesn't get spread out as much. Egg whites should be whipped in a smaller bowl, as they don't whip as quickly in a large one. Ultimately, you want the ingredients to fit in the bowl, but not to spill out of it.

Mixer

Another holy grail item in the macaron kitchen is an electric mixer. I started off with an electric hand mixer, and once it became too tiring, I invested in a stand mixer. I still use a hand mixer for smaller jobs, such as making cake batter or small amounts of buttercream or macarons. However, large quantities are best made with a stand mixer, which is well worth the cost. If you're just starting out, you can definitely start with a less expensive hand mixer. I recommend KitchenAid for both hand and stand mixers, both of which have lasted me for years.

Silicone/Plastic Spatula

I once thought that silicone spatulas weren't absolutely necessary to make macarons, until I tried folding macaron batter with a wooden spoon. The rounded shape of the wooden spoon made it difficult to mix the batter, so I switched to a flat silicone spatula and never looked back. The flat surface helps fold the batter easily, while the silicone construction is flexible and comfortable to hold in your hand. I do not recommend a metal spatula to mix batter or to remove baked macarons from silicone mats.

Pastry Bag and Tips

When I started making macarons, I thought I could just spoon the batter onto parchment paper. Boy, was I wrong! Those macarons turned out as flat, misshapen blobs! A pastry bag with a round tip creates evenly distributed batter in perfect circles. Reusable piping bags (or pastry bags) are great because you can use them repeatedly. I also sometimes use disposable bags, because I like to see the color of the batter peeking through, then I wash them with soap and water after each use. After a while, the bags develop holes, so you have to throw them away eventually. Normally, I use reusable piping bags for buttercream/fillings, and disposable bags for macaron batter, as butter can make the disposable bags greasy. For piping shells, I recommend a Wilton #12 tip, but I don't usually use a tip for filling. If you want to be fancy, you can use a star tip to make a pretty effect for the buttercream.

Silicone Macaron Baking Mat

Silicone macaron baking mats are also important for baking macarons. Many types are available, including those with pre-drawn circle templates, making it easy to create uniform macarons. I recommend the Amazon Basics silicone macaron baking mats. As a backup, you can also use parchment paper (not wax paper; the cookies will stick). If you use parchment paper, you can draw circles on the back of the paper using a food coloring pen. (You can print out a template on my blog; see the Resources on page 200.) That said, I prefer not to use parchment paper because it will take the shape of the pan. If the pan is warped, the macaron batter you piped will be warped, too. Silicone mats usually keep their shape.

Half-Sheet Pan

An 13-by-18-inch (half-sheet) aluminum sheet pan is a wise investment for your macaron kitchen. You can use these half-sheet pans to bake anything, and they fit perfectly in most conventional ovens. You can also use any sheet pan you have available, but I find that half-sheet pans are best because they are mostly flat. If macarons bake on an uneven surface, unsurprisingly, they bake unevenly.

Oven Thermometer

Internal oven thermometers can be completely off, or off by a little bit. As a precise baking temperature is essential for successful macarons, I highly recommend purchasing an oven thermometer. My home oven temperature fluctuates by as much as 50°F, which can be detrimental for macarons. You can adjust your oven accordingly by increments of 5°F.

Electric Fan/Dehumidifier

An electric fan and dehumidifier are worthy investments if you live in a humid area. Sometimes, macarons can take up to 3 hours or more to form a skin—or they may not dry at all. A medium-size electric fan will speed the drying process so the macarons do not crack when baked. If the environment is humid, a dehumidifier will help absorb the water from the air around the macarons, helping dry the shells.

Sifter

A sifter is a necessary item for smooth, beautiful macaron shells. Although almond flour is finely ground, it sometimes has large chunks that you don't want in your batter. Sifting helps eliminate those lumps. If, after sifting, large chunks remain, either pulse them in a food processor and sift again, or throw them away.

INVEST IN YOUR MACARON SUCCESS

If you love macarons enough to buy this book, investing in some good equipment will help you make them perfectly! If funds are limited, there are just a few must-have items to consider: a digital scale for correct measurements, a sifter for beautiful shells, a piping bag and tip for uniformly round macarons, an electric mixer for ease, half-sheet pan, and silicone macaron baking mats for a level baking surface.

YOUR MACARON BUILDING BLOCKS

A macaron shell is made of five simple ingredients: almond flour, powdered sugar, granulated sugar, salt, and egg whites. Each ingredient plays a specific role in developing the perfect macaron, and due to the structure of the recipe, substitutes can only be made for the egg whites and almond flour. Additional ingredients, such as butter, coloring, flavoring, and those needed for the filling, also play a part. Let's break it down.

Almond Flour

Almond flour plays a huge role in a macaron's taste and texture. Almond flour is, essentially, blanched almonds finely ground to the texture of a flour or powder. Almond meal is coarsely ground and contains almond skins. If you use almond meal instead of almond flour in a macaron recipe, the texture will be lumpier, as well as have almond skin specks. However, if you can't find almond flour, grind blanched slivered almonds in a food processor with the powdered sugar called for in a recipe (to absorb the excess oil) into a powder, then sift it to remove any lumps. To keep almond flour fresh, refrigerate it. You can also store it in an airtight container at a temperature below 70°F. If stored above that temperature, the almond flour may start to release natural oils and negatively affect your macarons.

Sugar

Sugar is the main building block of the chemical structure of macarons. The two types of sugar, powdered and granulated, help create the ruffle at the bottom (the "foot") and the smooth shell on top.

Powdered sugar, or confectioners' sugar, is finely ground sugar that has cornstarch in it. It helps dry the macaron batter to create the smooth shell. Once dry, the batter rises underneath to create the ruffle at the bottom, also called the foot, or *pied* in French. I've tried replacing powdered sugar with powdered stevia (noncaloric sweetener) and the results were not good. As of this writing, I don't know of any powdered sugar substitute that can be used in macaron recipes.

Granulated sugar, or cane sugar, is what creates the meringue. When whipped with egg whites, granulated sugar binds with the protein structures to stabilize it. I have also tried to make a meringue with stevia, but this didn't turn out well, either.

Salt

Salt is an optional ingredient in most recipes, but because macarons contain more sugar than other desserts, I prefer to add salt to offset that sweetness for sensitive palates. I use kosher salt, but you can use regular table salt as well. Sea salt is a little too grainy for macarons.

Egg Whites

Egg whites are the last key ingredient to making successful macarons, but extra care must be taken when separating the whites from the yolks. Egg whites provide the leavening element. When whipped, they create a light, fluffy meringue that is folded into the almond flour and powdered sugar. The best time to whip egg whites is when they are at room temperature, because the egg white proteins are relaxed. However, they will whip up whether they are cold or at room temperature.

SEPARATING EGG WHITES

Separating egg whites can be a bit tricky. Before starting, I like to grab two small bowls—one for the whites and one for the yolks. I crack one egg on the side of a metal or glass bowl (not plastic) in the center of the eggshell, so it breaks evenly. When the crack has encompassed most of the egg, I use both hands to separate the two halves, holding the intact yolk in one half shell, and begin moving the egg yolk back and forth between the shells over one small bowl to collect the egg whites. Once most of the white is collected, I use my hands to grab any excess egg white and drop it into the bowl. I place the yolk into the other bowl and compost the eggshell. There are egg separator devices available, but I haven't found any that I like, as some egg whites still get stuck in the separator. I prefer to make sure all the egg white is used and not wasted. You can use the extra egg yolks to make scrambled eggs, steamed egg custard, ice cream, or Crème Brûlée Custard Buttercream (page 187).

WEIGHING EGG WHITES

After you've separated the egg whites, you'll need to weigh them. It may be a learning curve, as they are quite thick and hard to pour. I've found the best tool to handle egg whites is your hand, because it's easier to separate the blobs with hands than with a spoon. Egg whites at room temperature become a bit more liquid and easier to pour. A rule of thumb is that one medium egg contains about 30 grams of egg whites, so in my basic recipe, you need about 2 eggs. There will be some white left over that you can refrigerate, covered, to save for the next batch.

To weigh your egg whites into the mixing bowl, put the bowl on the scale and tare it (see Weigh the Ingredients, page 13). Then, pour in the amount of egg whites called for. If you overpour, you can easily remove extra by grabbing the white, pinching it with your hand to separate, and placing it back in the original egg white bowl.

For convenience, use the table on page 10 to determine roughly how many eggs you will need based on the weight of egg whites required in any particular recipe.

AGING EGG WHITES

"Aging" egg whites is the process of separating egg whites, covering them in plastic wrap, and leaving them out at room temperature to evaporate some of the egg white liquid. Many people swear by aging their egg whites, saying that it helps dry out their macarons faster, but in my experience, it hasn't made much of a difference. I use eggs straight out of the refrigerator, and they turn out fine. If the area you live in is hot and humid, I would recommend trying it to see if it reduces the drying time.

EGG SIZES AND WEIGHTS

US EGG SIZE	APPROXIMATE EGG WHITE WEIGHT (GRAMS)
Small	15 to 25
Medium	25 to 30
Large	30 to 40
Extra Large	40 to 50
Jumbo	50 to 60

Flavor Extracts

Without flavoring, a macaron shell tastes like almond and vanilla with sugar. Flavorings make macarons more exciting, and they can be purchased online or in many grocery stores. Higher-quality extract delivers better-tasting flavor, whereas lower-quality options will taste artificial, or like alcohol. There are some interesting flavor combinations out there. I prefer not to add flavoring to some shells, especially in recipes that contain most of the flavor in the filling. If you use extract, do not add too much, as it can affect the batter and make it too runny. My favorite extracts include almond, lemon, mint, and vanilla.

Food Colorings

Liquid food colorings are available in the baking aisle of every grocery store, but when it comes to macarons, use gel or powdered food colorings for both the macaron shells and the filling. Liquid food colorings are diluted with water, so the color is not strong and you'll have to add many drops to get the desired color. This can make the macaron batter too runny. I recommend AmeriColor, ChefMaster, and The Sugar Art brands, which offer great pigmented gel and powdered food coloring in many shades. I prefer gel over powder due to the ease of use and their better colors. However, do not add too much gel coloring, either, or your macarons will not dry.

INGREDIENTS FOR VEGAN
AND NUT-FREE MACARONS

If you choose to make the vegan or nut-free macaron recipes in this book, you'll need to know about two fundamental ingredients, which take a little more preparation and care to ensure they work well in the recipes.

Canned chickpeas: Although you will need a whole can of chickpeas to make vegan macarons, you will use only the liquid from the can. This liquid, called aquafaba, has the unique capacity to whip up like egg whites when beaten with granulated sugar. A 15-ounce can of chickpeas will yield about 75 grams of aquafaba; a 28-ounce can yields about 150 grams of aquafaba.

Sunflower seed flour or oat flour: Nut-free macarons can be made with either sunflower seed flour or oat flour. Sunflower seed flour is made by grinding shelled sunflower seeds with powdered sugar (as called for in a recipe) in a food processor, similar to making your own almond flour (see page 7). Oat flour is made by grinding rolled oats in a food processor in the same way. Oat flour is a bit more subtle in flavor than sunflower seed flour, so the choice depends on your taste preferences.

Butter

Butter is another crucial ingredient in macarons and the main ingredient in butter-cream filling. Butter should be unsalted and at room temperature before using—the butter will be soft as you squish it in the wrapper, and a knife will slide through the butter easily. Butter also needs to be whipped to a light and creamy texture to avoid a buttery taste. If your butter has just come out of the refrigerator, leave it on the counter for at least 2 hours until you can slide a knife through it easily. Or, microwave 1 stick (113 grams) straight out of the refrigerator, on a plate, for 18 seconds on high power.

White Chocolate/Semisweet Chocolate

For some filling recipes in this book, you will need white and semisweet chocolate. Avoid white chocolate chips, because they tend to contain a lot of additives. I prefer Callebaut white chocolate callets for the best taste; you can also use Ghirardelli white melting wafers. For semisweet chocolate, chips are acceptable to use.

Freeze-Dried Fruit

Many of the fruity filling and macaron shell recipes in this book use freeze-dried fruit, which can be a little expensive, but in the long run, saves money and time because the fruit stays fresh longer. Additionally, freeze-dried fruit provides more concentrated flavor as it's not diluted with water, like fresh fruit. Freeze-dried fruit can be found at many grocery stores, Target, Trader Joe's, and online.

MACARONS: STEP BY STEP

Making macaron shells can seem difficult at first, but I break it down into detailed, manageable steps. Each step is essential, but remember that you don't need to rush when making macarons. Take your time and do it right, and you will be rewarded for your patience with beautiful, delicious macarons. There are some new techniques here, so the following steps include my best tips and tricks on how to perform them.

1. Weigh the Ingredients

Using a kitchen scale is really very simple. Digital kitchen scales have a "tare" feature. "Tare" means to zero out the scale so you can weigh the ingredients minus the weight of the vessel you put them in (the bowl, for example). You need the bowl to measure the ingredients, but you don't want the bowl's weight to count in the weight of the ingredients. You tare the scale so it will start over and only give the weight of the ingredients. To weigh almond flour and powdered sugar, place a small or medium bowl on the scale and turn the scale on. If it's not at zero, tare it. Then, using a spoon, portion the almond flour, powdered sugar, and salt together into the bowl until you have the amount you need. Then, tare the bowl that you'll use for the egg whites, then crack and separate the eggs, putting the yolks into a separate bowl for another use. Use a small bowl to weigh the granulated sugar the same way.

2. Combine the Dry Ingredients

Grab a sifter and place it inside or over another small or medium bowl. Pour the almond flour, powdered sugar, and salt into the sifter and turn the handle to keep sifting. If any large pieces remain in the sifter, either use a spoon to push them through, set aside for grinding, or discard.

3. Whip the Egg Whites into a French Meringue

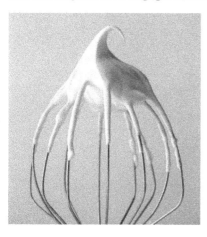

French meringue is an integral component of macarons. If using a hand mixer, you can use the same bowl you weighed the egg whites in. Otherwise, transfer the egg whites to the bowl of a stand mixer. Whip the egg whites on medium-high speed for about 2 minutes until frothy, like a bubble bath, then gradually pour in the granulated sugar. Turn the mixer to high speed and whip the egg whites for 3 to 4 minutes until stiff peaks form. To test their readiness, the egg whites should have thickened and whitened, and when you lift the beaters, stiff peaks hold that do not drip or run.

4. Complete the Macaronage

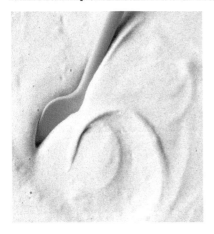

In batches, use a silicone spatula to fold the dry ingredients into the meringue, beating some air out of it. This process, called the macaronage, is important because if you overmix the batter, you will have flat macarons, and if you undermix the batter, the shells can crack or be lumpy. I like to rotate the bowl as I fold, and with every rotation, I fold and scrape the batter with the spatula, getting underneath it so everything gets combined, until the batter starts to come together and looks smoother. To test whether the batter is ready, pick up your spatula from the batter and see how slowly the batter flows into the bowl. It should flow in a continuous stream, but not too quickly. The batter should fall off the spatula in unbroken ribbons; some bakers compare it to flowing lava or a thick, flowing cake batter.

5. Pipe the Batter

When your batter is ready, line a 13-by-18-inch baking sheet with a silicone macaron baking mat or parchment paper and set it aside. (I highly recommend using a silicone mat with a circle template; otherwise make a circle template at home, or print one you find online, like the one on my blog. See Resources, page 200.) Then, grab a piping bag, Wilton #12 tip, and a wide mug to rest the bag in while you fill it with batter. I prefer to use Wilton disposable bags, because they are transparent, and #12 piping tips; however, you can also use a reusable piping bag and your tip of choice.

If you're using a reusable bag, simply drop the tip into the bag and unroll it into the mug. If using a disposable bag, cut off the end of the bag just enough to hold the tip, and drop the piping tip in. Use your spatula to help pour the batter into the bag, roll up the sides again, and twist the top, so no batter comes out from the top while piping.

Using a piping bag can be a little difficult at first, but hopefully this technique will help: Use your dominant hand to hold the piping bag twisted at the top, and your nondominant hand to hold the bag at the bottom. Using the template on the macaron mat, position your piping bag right above the first circle and squeeze with your dominant hand to pipe the circle. When it is almost 1½ inches in diameter, stop and flick your wrist to the side so the macaron shell ends without a peak on top. Fill the whole tray, then use your hand or the countertop to hit the bottom of the pan until the macarons flatten a little and any peaks disappear, but not too much so the circles become completely flat (two or three times should be fine).

6. Rest the Batter

After the macarons have been piped, they need to rest, or dry, until the shells are not sticky or shiny. If you don't allow for resting, there is a higher chance of cracking, as the shells will rise unevenly, instead of from the bottom, where the foot is formed. When the macarons dry, it creates a barrier so they do not crack when rising in the oven. Usually, macarons take about 30 minutes to 1 hour to dry fully, but in humid climates or rainy weather, it can take longer. To speed up the drying process, use a fan or a dehumidifier and check the macarons every 15 minutes. To make sure the macarons are dry, they should appear dull instead of shiny, and if you touch one, it won't stick to your finger or feel too soft when pushed on lightly. It should be a bit solid. Keep an eye on the macarons, and when they are almost dry, position a rack in the center of the oven and preheat the oven to the required temperature.

7. Bake the Macaron Shells

Use an oven thermometer to make sure your oven temperature is correct. Bake the macarons on the center rack for 12 to 14 minutes, depending on the heat of your oven. If it's hotter than usual, bake for 12 minutes; if it's normal, then 14 minutes. There is no need to rotate the pan unless your oven has uneven heat. If you are worried about the macarons getting browned in the oven, you can either add white food coloring or place an empty pan on the top rack to shield the cookies from direct heat. The shells are done when you tap them and they move very slightly, and the feet have fallen a bit, so the shells don't look too puffy.

8. Cool the Shells

After baking, cool the shells on a wire rack (so air can flow underneath the pan) for 15 to 30 minutes. You don't want to fill macarons when they are still warm, because their heat will melt the filling. Once cool, carefully remove the shells from the mats or parchment paper by pulling up a corner of the mat/parchment and peeling it away from the macaron, instead of the other way around. Another tip is to take both diagonal corners of the mat or parchment and flip it on the other side so the macarons are facing down. Then, use both hands to slowly peel away the mat/parchment from the macarons. If the shells are sticky at all and hard to remove, then they are slightly underbaked, but that is better than being overbaked.

9. Make the Filling

While the macarons cool, make the filling as directed in the recipe. If you're making a buttercream, make sure the butter is at room temperature before you start. Fillings can also be made in advance, and leftovers can be refrigerated, covered, for up to 2 weeks, or frozen for up to 2 months. If made in advance, remove the filling from the freezer the morning you'll use it and let it thaw to room temperature. In fact, any of the ganaches must be made in advance.

10. Fill the Shells

Get a piping bag (no tip required) and unroll it as you did when filling it with batter. Spoon some filling into the piping bag, roll it up, and twist it as in step 5. Hold a macaron shell in your non-dominant hand, then use the piping bag to swirl or dollop a half-dollar–size amount of butter-cream in the center of the foot side of the shell. If doing a swirl, start from the outside of the shell and finish inside with a flick of the wrist. If doing a dollop, start in the middle and end higher up. I prefer my filling a bit thick, so I hold my piping bag slightly farther away from the shell than I do the pan for piping macaron batter. Then, use a matching shell to close it by twisting them together, feet facing in, making sure the feet line up. This prevents the filling from escaping the sides of the shell.

11. Store the Filled Macarons

I recommend refrigerating the just-filled macarons for at least 1 hour (but preferably 24 hours) and then let them come to room temperature before serving, so the flavors meld. Macarons are best enjoyed within 4 to 5 days of baking. Refrigerate filled macarons in an airtight container. They also freeze well for up to 2 months. Macarons cannot be left at room temperature for more than a day, or they start to get dry and hard. Unfilled macaron shells can also be refrigerated for up to 3 days, and frozen for up to 2 weeks.

MACARONS GONE WRONG: A TROUBLESHOOTING GUIDE

PROBLEM	THE LIKELY CAUSE(S)	THE FIX(ES)
Bottom not attached/no bottom	• Not letting macarons cool long enough before removing from the mat • Not baking long enough • Oven temperature too low	• Let the shells cool long enough so they are not warm to the touch; use a fan to speed the process. • Bake the shells long enough. • Use an oven thermometer and adjust the temperature accordingly.
Browned shells	• Oven temperature too hot • Baking too long • Not using white food coloring	• Use an oven thermometer and adjust the temperature accordingly. • Bake a few minutes less. • Use white food coloring.
Buttercream is lumpy	• Butter was too cold • Milk was too cold	• Make sure the butter is very soft before using. • Use room-temperature milk so there is no difference in temperature and the butter doesn't firm up.
Buttercream separated	• Buttercream was not whipped long enough • Too much liquid in the buttercream	• Whip buttercream on high speed so the butter and liquid come together. • Do not add more than the recommended amount of liquid. • Add more powdered sugar to soak up the liquid.

PROBLEM	THE LIKELY CAUSE(S)	THE FIX(ES)
Cracked shells	• Shells did not dry long enough • Batter was overmixed • Batter was undermixed • Oven temperature too hot • Underwhipped meringue • Too much food coloring	• Let shells dry until they are dull and not sticky. • Do not overmix or undermix the batter; make sure it flows continuously, but slowly. • Use an oven thermometer and adjust the temperature accordingly. • Make sure your meringue reaches stiff peaks when beaten. • Do not add more than 4 drops of food coloring to the batter.
Exploded/spread feet	• Oven temperature too hot • Batter was overmixed	• Use an oven thermometer and adjust the temperature accordingly. • Do not overmix the batter; make sure it flows continuously, but slowly.
Flat, crispy shells	• Batter was overmixed • Too much food coloring	• Do not overmix or undermix the batter; make sure it flows continuously, but slowly. • Do not add more than 4 drops of food coloring to the batter.
Fragile, soft shells	• Oily almond flour • Underwhipped meringue • Not baking long enough	• Buy almond flour that isn't too oily (see page 3), or dry it in the oven at 150°F for 20 minutes. • Make sure your meringue reaches stiff peaks when beaten. • Bake the shells a little longer, until they don't move when you touch them, or adjust your oven temperature.

PROBLEM	THE LIKELY CAUSE(S)	THE FIX(ES)
Ganache is lumpy	• Chocolate not melted	• Melt the chocolate longer.
Ganache is separated	• Ganache heated too long • Ganache not mixed enough	• Don't overheat the meringue over a double boiler; heat only until it is combined. • If this happens, keep whisking until the ganache comes back together.
Hollow shells	• Not baking long enough • Oven temperature too hot or too low • Batter was overmixed or undermixed • Shells rested too long • Improper macaronage technique (see page 14)	• Use an oven thermometer and adjust the temperature accordingly. • Bake the shells a little longer, until they don't move when you touch them. • Do not overmix or undermix the batter; make sure it flows continuously, but slowly. • Do not rest the shells longer than 3 to 4 hours.
Lopsided shells	• Shells rested too long • Oven temperature is uneven	• Do not rest the shells longer than 3 to 4 hours. • Rotate the pan every 5 minutes while baking if your heat is uneven.
Lumpy shells	• Batter was undermixed • Dry ingredients not sifted • Lumpy almond flour	• Do not overmix or undermix the batter; make sure it flows continuously, but slowly. • Sift the dry ingredients. • Use a finer grit almond flour, or grind it in a food processor with powdered sugar to soak up any excess oil.

PROBLEM	THE LIKELY CAUSE(S)	THE FIX(ES)
Misshapen shells	• Using warped baking trays • Using parchment paper • Batter was overmixed	• Use trays that are not warped. • Use silicone mats. • Do not overmix the batter; make sure it flows continuously, but slowly.
Oil spots on shells or wrinkled shells	• Oily almond flour • Overwhipped meringue • Too much cocoa or matcha powder added	• Buy almond flour that isn't too oily (see page 3), or dry it in the oven at 150°F for 20 minutes. • Do not overwhip the meringue past stiff peaks, where it deflates. • Do not add more than the recommended amounts of cocoa or matcha powder.
Porous shells	• Underwhipped meringue • Too much food coloring • Broken meringue • Oily almond flour	• Make sure your meringue reaches stiff peaks when beaten. • Do not add more than 4 drops of food coloring to the batter. • Do not overwhip your meringue or let it sit too long that it deflates. • Buy almond flour that isn't too oily (see page 3), or dry it in the oven at 150°F for 20 minutes.
Ruffled feet	• Batter was overmixed • Overwhipped meringue • Oven temperature too hot	• Do not overmix or undermix the batter; make sure it flows continuously, but slowly. • Do not overwhip the meringue past stiff peaks, where it deflates. • Use an oven thermometer and adjust the temperature accordingly.

PROBLEM	THE LIKELY CAUSE(S)	THE FIX(ES)
Shells didn't develop feet	• Shells did not dry long enough • Batter was overmixed • Batter was undermixed • Oven temperature too low • Shells rested too long	• Let shells dry until they are dull and not sticky. • Do not overmix or undermix the batter; make sure it flows continuously, but slowly. • Use an oven thermometer and adjust the temperature accordingly. • Do not rest the shells longer than 3 to 4 hours.
Shells with air bubbles	• Trays were not tapped to get rid of air bubbles • Overwhipped meringue • Improper macaronage technique (see page 14)	• Make sure you hit the tray to remove air bubbles, or pop any with a toothpick before letting the shells dry. • Do not overwhip the meringue past stiff peaks, where it deflates. • Do not overmix or undermix the batter; make sure it flows continuously, but slowly.

STEPPING UP YOUR MACARON GAME

Once you've mastered the basic macaron, you'll want to advance to the next level—creative designs, unique shapes, and fun flavors! Macarons make great gifts for friends and family, and can be packaged or displayed in beautiful and whimsical ways. Check out chapter 4 (page 107) for holiday and celebration macarons. In this section, you'll get fun ideas to take your skills up a notch.

Shapeshifters

Other than circles, macarons can be made into the shapes of your favorite things or cute characters! The easiest shape to start with is a bear (see page 134)—all you have to do is add two small round circles (ears) to the basic round macaron. You can even make or print templates (see the Resources section, page 200) to make measurements even more precise. I suggest starting with the easier characters and working up to more complex ones. As the macaron batter dries, you can add more layers as well, creating a 3-D effect.

The Rainbow's the Limit

As you build your collection of gel food colorings, you can make almost any color of the rainbow! But even if you don't have a lot of colors, you can mix individual colors to create the ones you want. To create a rainbow swirl effect, divide the batter into smaller bowls before it's fully mixed, then add different food colorings to each bowl and finish mixing.

For example, using your spatula, pour one color of batter on one side of the piping bag and scrape off the remaining on the edge of the cup. Repeat with a second color on another side, and, finally, pour a third color of batter on the last side of the piping bag to create a swirl effect. The batter will naturally fall in place together, and when you pipe the batter, it will come out in a three-color design.

The Decorated Macaron

Aside from cool shapes and beautiful colors, you can also decorate macarons with different mediums to produce different effects! My (and my customers') favorites include gold dusting, brushing, or splatter work on the shells to create a sophisticated, luxe look. You can also paint them with edible food paint, or airbrush a stencil onto them. Another favorite option is to use royal icing to create 3-D effects that aren't possible with macaron batter, or to use an edible food coloring pen to add small details.

It's All in the Presentation

One of the best features of macarons is that they are petite and fit nicely in displays or in favor boxes. Many people use macarons as wedding favors, or even wedding displays on a tower. These displays can be purchased online at an affordable price. If you are doing favor boxes, I recommend using clear plastic 2-inch square boxes, with a ribbon or bow to make the presentation even more festive. Macaron towers elevate the look of an event with their visual appeal. For less lavish but still festive gifting, I like to use macaron boxes that have dividers. Alternately, you can use crinkled tissue paper to pad the macarons in a box so they don't bounce around in transit.

THE RECIPES

The recipes in this book are broken down into five sections for easier reading. For a more precise result, I only use weight measurements instead of volume. Each chapter begins with the most basic flavors or concepts, and recipes are grouped by theme, ingredients, or complexity/decadence, in ascending order.

We'll begin with **The Classics**, which include the traditional pâtisserie offerings, such as chocolate, pistachio, rose, vanilla, and more. These macaron varieties are commonly found at French bakeries, and I suggest you start with these before trying anything more complicated, to get the hang of it.

Next, **New Creations** tackles fun and unique flavors. Some recipes may sound new to you, but I encourage you to "step outside the macaron box" and try them. The most exciting part of this book, though, is the **Holidays and Celebrations** chapter, where I describe how to make fun, shaped macarons like snowmen, bears, turkeys, and more! Another great topic is **Vegan and Nut-Free Macarons and Fillings**, for those who follow a plant-based diet or have a nut allergy. We'll explore how to create these treats along with flavor variations and fillings. Think of these recipes as a template you can work from to make the macarons your own. Lastly, **Fillings** includes all the filling recipes used in the previous chapters' macaron recipes.

Because the real excitement of making macarons is the endless flavor combinations, every macaron recipe includes a **Change It Up** tip, which suggests alternative fillings that pair well with that particular shell. Each filling recipe also includes a **Perfect Partners** tip, suggesting which shells match well with it.

Although the recipes include fairly detailed instructions, I recommend referring back to the step-by-step instructions (see page 13) for more guidance if you're just starting out, or want a refresher.

Doubling Up or Cutting in Half

My macaron shell recipes make at least 12 filled macarons. I don't recommend cutting any recipe in half, or the proportions may not work properly. The filling recipes, however, make a little more than enough to fill 12 completed macarons, so you could halve these recipes if needed. All recipes can be doubled if you'd like to make more than the original recipe yields. Macarons are built on proper proportions, and as long as you maintain the ratios, they will turn out correctly (and deliciously) when scaling up.

Lemon Macarons page 32

CHAPTER 2

The Classics

Vanilla Macaron 28

Chocolate Macarons 30

Lemon Macarons 32

Strawberry Macarons 34

Raspberry Macarons 36

Mango Macarons 38

Chocolate Mint Macarons 40

Toasted Almond Macarons 42

Pistachio Macarons 44

Earl Grey Macarons 46

Matcha Green Tea Macarons 48

Honey Lavender Macarons 50

Rose Macarons 52

Red Velvet Macarons 54

Mocha Macarons 56

Espresso Macarons 58

Salted Caramel Macarons 60

Tiramisu Macarons 62

VANILLA MACARONS

PREP TIME: 30 minutes, plus 30 minutes to 2 hours to dry and 1 hour to refrigerate
BAKE TIME: 14 minutes
MAKES: 12 to 15 filled 1½-inch macarons

Once you master this simple recipe, you'll want to branch out into different flavors. You'll also experience how a macaron should taste in its purest form: sweet, chewy, and light. These macarons have a subtle taste of almond and vanilla, making them a sweet snack any time of day. Optional white food coloring helps ensure the treats don't brown.

70 grams almond flour

50 grams powdered sugar

Pinch salt

53 grams egg whites (from about 2 medium eggs)

50 grams granulated sugar

1 gram (¼ teaspoon) vanilla extract

2 drops white gel food coloring (optional)

1 recipe Vanilla Buttercream (page 164)

1. Sift the almond flour, powdered sugar, and salt into a small to medium bowl. Set aside.

2. In another small to medium bowl, with an electric mixer on medium-high speed, beat the egg whites for 1 to 2 minutes until frothy. While beating on medium-high speed, slowly add the granulated sugar, then beat on high speed for about 3 minutes until the mixture is thicker and white. Add the vanilla and food coloring (if using) and beat for 3 to 4 minutes until the meringue is thick, with firm, glossy peaks when you lift the beaters. Turn the bowl upside down; if the meringue does not move, it is ready. If not, whip in 1- to 2-minute increments until stiff peaks form.

3. With a silicone spatula, fold one-third of the almond flour mixture into the meringue until just combined. In two batches, fold in the remaining almond flour mixture. The batter should flow off the spatula, slowly but continuously, in unbroken ribbons.

4. Line a 13-by-18-inch baking sheet with a silicone macaron baking mat or parchment paper.

5. Transfer the batter to a pastry bag fitted with a Wilton #12 round tip. Pipe 24 to 30 (1½-inch) circles onto the prepared baking sheet, 1 to 1½ inches apart. Gently drop the baking sheet on the counter to eliminate air bubbles and level the macarons. Dry the macarons at room temperature for 30 minutes to 2 hours, uncovered, until dull, firm, not sticky, and dry to the touch.

6. When the macarons look almost ready, position a rack in the center of the oven and preheat the oven to 300°F.

7. Bake the macarons on the center rack for 12 to 14 minutes, or until a macaron tapped on top moves only slightly.

8. Let cool on a wire rack for 15 to 30 minutes, then transfer the macarons to another tray to match similar-size shells.

9. Fill as directed in the filling recipe. Top each filled shell with another shell, then press and twist the shells together.

10. Remove from the refrigerator 30 minutes before serving.

CHANGE IT UP: Fill with Cookies and Cream Buttercream (page 175), Crème Brûlée Custard Buttercream (page 187), or Toasted Almond Buttercream (page 189).

CHOCOLATE MACARONS

PREP TIME: 30 minutes, plus 30 minutes to 2 hours to dry and 1 hour to refrigerate
BAKE TIME: 14 minutes
MAKES: 12 to 15 filled 1½-inch macarons

Calling all chocolate lovers—this is *your* macaron recipe! The chewiness of the macaron shell paired with the rich chocolate buttercream filling really makes this a decadent treat.

70 grams almond flour

45 grams powdered sugar

5 grams unsweetened
  cocoa powder

Pinch salt

53 grams egg whites (from
  about 2 medium eggs)

50 grams granulated sugar

2 or 3 drops brown gel food
  coloring

1 recipe Chocolate
  Buttercream (page 165)

1. Sift the almond flour, powdered sugar, cocoa powder, and salt into a small to medium bowl. Set aside.

2. In another small to medium bowl, with an electric mixer on medium-high speed, beat the egg whites for 1 to 2 minutes until frothy. While beating on medium-high speed, slowly add the granulated sugar, then beat on high speed for about 3 minutes until the mixture is thicker and white. Add the food coloring and beat on high speed for 3 to 4 minutes until the meringue is thick, with firm, glossy peaks when you lift the beaters. Turn the bowl upside down; if the meringue does not move, it is ready. If not, whip in 1- to 2-minute increments until stiff peaks form.

3. With a silicone spatula, fold one-third of the almond flour mixture into the meringue until just combined. In two batches, fold in the remaining almond flour mixture. The batter should flow off the spatula, slowly but continuously, in unbroken ribbons.

4. Line a 13-by-18-inch baking sheet with a silicone macaron baking mat or parchment paper.

5. Transfer the batter to a pastry bag fitted with a Wilton #12 round tip. Pipe 24 to 30 (1½-inch) circles onto the prepared baking sheet, 1 to 1½ inches apart. Gently drop the baking sheet on the counter to eliminate air bubbles and level the macarons. Dry the macarons at room temperature for 30 minutes to 2 hours, uncovered, until dull, firm, not sticky, and dry to the touch.

6. When the macarons look almost ready, position a rack in the center of the oven and preheat the oven to 300°F.

7. Bake the macarons on the center rack for 12 to 14 minutes, or until a macaron tapped on top moves only slightly.

8. Let cool for 15 to 30 minutes on a wire rack, then transfer the macarons to another tray to match similar-size shells

9. Fill as directed in the filling recipe. Top each filled shell with another shell, then press and twist the shells together.

10. Remove from the refrigerator 30 minutes before serving.

CHANGE IT UP: Fill with Mocha Ganache (page 193), Espresso Buttercream (page 183), or Salted Caramel Buttercream (page 178).

LEMON MACARONS

PREP TIME: 30 minutes, plus 30 minutes to 2 hours to dry and 1 hour to refrigerate
BAKE TIME: 14 minutes
MAKES: 12 to 15 filled 1½-inch macarons

The tangy lemon in the macaron shells and buttercream delivers a zing to your taste buds. For this recipe, I use lemon extract for convenience; however, you can use 1 gram (⅛ teaspoon) grated lemon zest instead, if you wish. These brightly flavored macarons will have you coming back for more!

70 grams almond flour

50 grams powdered sugar

Pinch salt

53 grams egg whites (from about 2 medium eggs)

50 grams granulated sugar

1 gram (¼ teaspoon) lemon extract

2 drops yellow gel food coloring

1 recipe Lemon Buttercream (page 167)

1. Sift the almond flour, powdered sugar, and salt into a small to medium bowl. Set aside.

2. In another small to medium bowl, with an electric mixer on medium-high speed, beat the egg whites for 1 to 2 minutes until frothy. While beating on medium-high speed, slowly add the granulated sugar, then beat on high speed for about 3 minutes until the mixture is thicker and white. Add the lemon extract and food coloring and beat for 3 to 4 minutes until the meringue is thick, with firm, glossy peaks when you lift the beaters. Turn the bowl upside down; if the meringue does not move, it is ready. If not, whip in 1- to 2-minute increments until stiff peaks form.

3. With a silicone spatula, fold one-third of the almond flour mixture into the meringue until just combined. In two batches, fold in the remaining almond flour mixture. The batter should flow off the spatula, slowly but continuously, in unbroken ribbons.

4. Line a 13-by-18-inch baking sheet with a silicone macaron baking mat or parchment paper.

5. Transfer the batter to a pastry bag fitted with a Wilton #12 round tip. Pipe 24 to 30 (1½-inch) circles onto the prepared baking sheet, 1 to 1½ inches apart. Gently drop the baking sheet on the counter to eliminate air bubbles and level the macarons. Dry the macarons at room temperature for 30 minutes to 2 hours, uncovered, until dull, firm, not sticky, and dry to the touch.

6. When the macarons look almost ready, position a rack in the center of the oven and preheat the oven to 300°F.

7. Bake the macarons on the center rack for 12 to 14 minutes, or until a macaron tapped on top moves only slightly.

8. Let cool for 15 to 30 minutes on a wire rack, then transfer the macarons to another tray to match similar-size shells.

9. Fill as directed in the filling recipe. Top each filled shell with another shell, then press and twist the shells together.

10. Remove from the refrigerator 30 minutes before serving.

CHANGE IT UP: Fill with Strawberry Buttercream (page 166), Honey Lavender Whipped White Chocolate Ganache (page 196), or Tea Whipped White Chocolate Ganache (page 195), made with Earl Grey tea.

STRAWBERRY MACARONS

PREP TIME: 30 minutes, plus 30 minutes to 2 hours to dry and 1 hour to refrigerate
BAKE TIME: 14 minutes
MAKES: 12 to 15 filled 1½-inch macarons

Strawberry macarons are the most crowd-pleasing macaron I've made to date! Most of my customers ask for at least one strawberry flavor in their order. The flavor of the freeze-dried strawberries in the shell and buttercream is a lush reminder of summer that can be enjoyed any time of year.

5 grams freeze-dried
   strawberries
70 grams almond flour
45 grams powdered sugar
Pinch salt
53 grams egg whites (from
   about 2 medium eggs)
50 grams granulated sugar
2 drops pink gel food coloring
1 recipe Strawberry
   Buttercream (page 166)

1. In a food processor, pulse the freeze-dried strawberries into a powder.

2. Sift the almond flour, powdered sugar, strawberry powder, and salt into a small to medium bowl. Set aside.

3. In another small to medium bowl, with an electric mixer on medium-high speed, beat the egg whites for 1 to 2 minutes until frothy. While beating on medium-high speed, slowly add the granulated sugar, then beat on high speed for about 3 minutes until the mixture is thicker and white. Add the food coloring and beat on high speed for 3 to 4 minutes until the meringue is thick, with firm, glossy peaks when you lift the beaters. Turn the bowl upside down; if the meringue does not move, it is ready. If not, whip in 1- to 2-minute increments until stiff peaks form.

4. With a silicone spatula, fold one-third of the almond flour mixture into the meringue until just combined. In two batches, fold in the remaining almond flour mixture. The batter should flow off the spatula, slowly but continuously, in unbroken ribbons.

5. Line a 13-by-18-inch baking sheet with a silicone macaron baking mat or parchment paper.

6. Transfer the batter to a pastry bag fitted with a Wilton #12 round tip. Pipe 24 to 30 (1½-inch) circles onto the prepared baking sheet, 1 to 1½ inches apart. Gently drop the baking sheet on the counter to eliminate air bubbles and level the macarons. Dry the macarons at room temperature for 30 minutes to 2 hours, uncovered, until dull, firm, not sticky, and dry to the touch.

7. When the macarons look almost ready, position a rack in the center of the oven and preheat the oven to 300°F.

8. Bake the macarons on the center rack for 12 to 14 minutes, or until a macaron tapped on top moves only slightly.

9. Let cool for 15 to 30 minutes on a wire rack, then transfer the macarons to another tray to match similar-size shells.

10. Fill as directed in the filling recipe. Top each filled shell with another shell, then press and twist the shells together.

11. Remove from the refrigerator 30 minutes before serving.

CHANGE IT UP: Fill with Lemon Buttercream (page 167), Matcha Buttercream (page 179), or Passion Fruit Guava Buttercream (page 169).

RASPBERRY MACARONS

PREP TIME: 30 minutes, plus 30 minutes to 2 hours to dry and 1 hour to refrigerate
BAKE TIME: 14 minutes
MAKES: 12 to 15 filled 1½-inch macarons

Raspberries are one of my favorite fruits, and my customers' as well. The tart but sweet taste pairs well with a lightly sweet macaron such as these, and a creamy, sweet ganache offsets the tartness of the raspberries. It's fun to color these macarons the color of raspberries using red food coloring.

5 grams freeze-dried
   raspberries
70 grams almond flour
45 grams powdered sugar
Pinch salt
53 grams egg whites (from
   about 2 medium eggs)
50 grams granulated sugar
2 drops red gel food coloring
1 recipe White Chocolate
   Ganache (with White
   Chocolate Raspberry
   variation; page 197)

1. In a food processor, pulse the freeze-dried raspberries into a powder.

2. Sift the almond flour, powdered sugar, raspberry powder, and salt into a small to medium bowl. Set aside.

3. In another small to medium bowl, with an electric mixer on medium-high speed, beat the egg whites for 1 to 2 minutes until frothy. While beating on medium-high speed, slowly add the granulated sugar, then beat on high speed for about 3 minutes until the mixture is thicker and white. Add the food coloring and beat for 3 to 4 minutes until the meringue is thick, with firm, glossy peaks when you lift the beaters. Turn the bowl upside down; if the meringue does not move, it is ready. If not, whip in 1- to 2-minute increments until stiff peaks form.

4. With a silicone spatula, fold one-third of the almond flour mixture into the meringue until just combined. In two batches, fold in the remaining almond flour mixture. The batter should flow off the spatula, slowly but continuously, in unbroken ribbons.

5. Line a 13-by-18-inch baking sheet with a silicone macaron baking mat or parchment paper.

6. Transfer the batter to a pastry bag fitted with a Wilton #12 round tip. Pipe 24 to 30 (1½-inch) circles onto the prepared baking sheet, 1 to 1½ inches apart. Gently drop the baking sheet on the counter to eliminate air bubbles and level the macarons. Dry the macarons at room temperature for 30 minutes to 2 hours, uncovered, until dull, firm, not sticky, and dry to the touch.

7. When the macarons look almost ready, position a rack in the center of the oven and preheat the oven to 300°F.

8. Bake the macarons on the center rack for 12 to 14 minutes, or until a macaron tapped on top moves only slightly.

9. Let cool for 15 to 30 minutes on a wire rack, then transfer the macarons to another tray to match similar-size shells.

10. Fill as directed in the filling recipe. Top each filled shell with another shell, then press and twist the shells together

11. Remove from the refrigerator 30 minutes before serving.

CHANGE IT UP: Fill with Chocolate Buttercream (page 165), Rose Buttercream (page 180), or Lemon Buttercream (page 167).

MANGO MACARONS

PREP TIME: 30 minutes, plus 30 minutes to 2 hours to dry and 1 hour to refrigerate
BAKE TIME: 14 minutes
MAKES: 12 to 15 filled 1½-inch macarons

Freeze-dried mango and mango extract deliver a punch in every bite of these delicious macarons. Fresh fruit has too much moisture to use here, plus the freeze-dried version delivers more flavor. Mango extract can be found at select stores or online. If you can find it, get the Butterfly brand from the Philippines.

5 grams freeze-dried mango

70 grams almond flour

45 grams powdered sugar

Pinch salt

53 grams egg whites (from about 2 medium eggs)

50 grams granulated sugar

1 gram (¼ teaspoon) mango extract

1 drop yellow gel food coloring

1 drop orange gel food coloring

1 recipe Mango Buttercream (page 168)

1. In a food processor, pulse the freeze-dried mangos into a powder.

2. Sift the almond flour, powdered sugar, mango powder, and salt into a small to medium bowl. Set aside.

3. In another small to medium bowl, with an electric mixer on medium-high speed, beat the egg whites for 1 to 2 minutes until frothy. While beating on medium-high speed, slowly add the granulated sugar, then beat on high speed for about 3 minutes until the mixture is thicker and white. Add the mango extract and food colorings and beat for 3 to 4 minutes until the meringue is thick, with firm, glossy peaks when you lift the beaters. Turn the bowl upside down; if the meringue does not move, it is ready. If not, whip in 1- to 2-minute increments until stiff peaks form.

4. With a silicone spatula, fold one-third of the almond flour mixture into the meringue until just combined. In two batches, fold in the remaining almond flour mixture. The batter should flow off the spatula, slowly but continuously, in unbroken ribbons.

5. Line a 13-by-18-inch baking sheet with a silicone macaron baking mat or parchment paper.

6. Transfer the batter to a pastry bag fitted with a Wilton #12 round tip. Pipe 24 to 30 (1½-inch) circles onto the prepared baking sheet, 1 to 1½ inches apart. Gently drop the baking sheet on the counter to eliminate air bubbles and level the macarons. Dry the macarons at room temperature for 30 minutes to 2 hours, uncovered, until dull, firm, not sticky, and dry to the touch.

7. When the macarons look almost ready, position a rack in the center of the oven and preheat the oven to 300°F.

8. Bake the macarons on the center rack for 12 to 14 minutes, or until a macaron tapped on top moves only slightly.

9. Let cool for 15 to 30 minutes on a wire rack, then transfer the macarons to another tray to match similar-size shells.

10. Fill as directed in the filling recipe. Top each filled shell with another shell, then press and twist the shells together.

11. Remove from the refrigerator 30 minutes before serving.

CHANGE IT UP: Fill with Strawberry Buttercream (page 166), Matcha Buttercream (page 179), or Passion Fruit Guava Buttercream (page 169).

CHOCOLATE MINT MACARONS

PREP TIME: 30 minutes, plus 30 minutes to 2 hours to dry and 1 hour to refrigerate
BAKE TIME: 14 minutes
MAKES: 12 to 15 filled 1½-inch macarons

The fresh flavor of mint pairs perfectly with the rich chocolate in this macaron recipe. It reminds me of Andes Crème de Menthe candies, one of my favorites growing up. To add some flair, I like to color these macaron shells mint green and brush them with edible silver paint.

70 grams almond flour

45 grams powdered sugar

5 grams unsweetened
  cocoa powder

Pinch salt

53 grams egg whites (from
  about 2 medium eggs)

50 grams granulated sugar

1 gram (¼ teaspoon)
  mint extract

1 drop green gel food coloring

1 recipe Chocolate Mint
  Ganache (page 194)

Silver edible paint, for
  decorating (optional)

1. Sift the almond flour, powdered sugar, cocoa powder, and salt into a small to medium bowl. Set aside.

2. In another small to medium bowl, with an electric mixer on medium-high speed, beat the egg whites for 1 to 2 minutes until frothy. While beating on medium-high speed, slowly add the granulated sugar, then beat on high speed for about 3 minutes until the mixture is thicker and white. Add the mint extract and food coloring and beat for 3 to 4 minutes until the meringue is thick, with firm, glossy peaks when you lift the beaters. Turn the bowl upside down; if the meringue does not move, it is ready. If not, whip in 1- to 2-minute increments until stiff peaks form.

3. With a silicone spatula, fold one-third of the almond flour mixture into the meringue until just combined. In two batches, fold in the remaining flour mixture. The batter should flow off the spatula, slowly but continuously, in unbroken ribbons.

4. Line a 13-by-18-inch baking sheet with a silicone macaron baking mat or parchment paper.

5. Transfer the batter to a pastry bag fitted with a Wilton #12 round tip. Pipe 24 to 30 (1½-inch) circles onto the prepared baking sheet, 1 to 1½ inches apart. Gently drop the baking sheet on the counter to eliminate air bubbles and level the macarons. Dry the macarons at room temperature for 30 minutes to 2 hours, uncovered, until dull, firm, not sticky, and dry to the touch.

6. When the macarons look almost ready, position a rack in the center of the oven and preheat the oven to 300°F.

7. Bake the macarons on the center rack for 12 to 14 minutes, or until a macaron tapped on top moves only slightly.

8. Let cool for 15 to 30 minutes on a wire rack, then transfer the macarons to another tray to match similar-size shells.

9. Fill as directed in the filling recipe. Top each filled shell with another shell, then press and twist the shells together.

10. With a food-safe paintbrush, create a brushstroke effect on the top of the macarons with edible paint (if using). Refrigerate for at least 1 hour, or overnight.

11. Remove from the refrigerator 30 minutes before serving.

CHANGE IT UP: Fill with Chocolate Buttercream (page 165), Cookies and Cream Buttercream (page 175), or Espresso Buttercream (page 183).

TOASTED ALMOND MACARONS

PREP TIME: 30 minutes, plus 30 minutes to 2 hours to dry and 1 hour to refrigerate
BAKE TIME: 14 minutes
MAKES: 12 to 15 filled 1½-inch macarons

This is a staple recipe to have in your collection, as toasted almond macarons are the purest form of macaron—one that accentuates the almond flavor. I like to place almond slices on top to give the cookies a prettier look, and to give it that toasted flavor. The almond extract brings out the natural sweetness of the almond flour in the macaron shells.

70 grams almond flour
50 grams powdered sugar
Pinch salt
53 grams egg whites (from about 2 medium eggs)
50 grams granulated sugar
1 gram (¼ teaspoon) almond extract
1½ teaspoons sliced almonds
1 recipe Toasted Almond Buttercream (page 189)

1. Sift the almond flour, powdered sugar, and salt into a small to medium bowl. Set aside.

2. In another small to medium bowl, with an electric mixer on medium-high speed, beat the egg whites for 1 to 2 minutes until frothy. While beating on medium-high speed, slowly add the granulated sugar, then beat on high speed for about 3 minutes until the mixture is thicker and white. Add the almond extract and beat for 3 to 4 minutes until the meringue is thick, with firm, glossy peaks when you lift the beaters. Turn the bowl upside down; if the meringue does not move, it is ready. If not, whip in 1- to 2-minute increments until stiff peaks form.

3. With a silicone spatula, fold one-third of the almond flour mixture into the meringue until just combined. In two batches, fold in the remaining almond flour mixture. The batter should flow off the spatula, slowly but continuously, in unbroken ribbons.

4. Line a 13-by-18-inch baking sheet with a silicone macaron baking mat or parchment paper.

5. Transfer the batter to a pastry bag fitted with a Wilton #12 round tip. Pipe 24 to 30 (1½-inch) circles onto the prepared baking sheet, 1 to 1½ inches apart. Gently drop the baking sheet on the counter to eliminate air bubbles and level the macarons. Evenly sprinkle the sliced almonds over the tops of the macaron shells. Dry the macarons at room temperature for 30 minutes to 2 hours, uncovered, until dull, firm, not sticky, and dry to the touch.

6. When the macarons look almost ready, position a rack in the center of the oven and preheat the oven to 300°F.

7. Bake the macarons on the center rack for 12 to 14 minutes, or until a macaron tapped on top moves only slightly.

8. Let cool for 15 to 30 minutes on a wire rack, then transfer the macarons to another tray to match similar-size shells.

9. Fill as directed in the filling recipe. Top each filled shell with another shell, then press and twist the shells together.

10. Remove from the refrigerator 30 minutes before serving.

CHANGE IT UP: Fill with Pistachio Buttercream (page 188), Cookie Butter Buttercream (page 174), or Rose Buttercream (page 180).

PISTACHIO MACARONS

PREP TIME: 30 minutes, plus 30 minutes to 2 hours to dry and 1 hour to refrigerate
BAKE TIME: 14 minutes
MAKES: 12 to 15 filled 1½-inch macarons

The roasted, nutty flavor of pistachio in macarons is a French classic. The nut's saltiness offsets any sweetness, which is wonderful for people who don't like overly sweet pastries. The chunkiness of the nuts in the buttercream adds great texture as well.

2 grams whole pistachios, plus 6 grams, finely ground
70 grams almond flour
48 grams powdered sugar
Pinch salt
53 grams egg whites (from about 2 medium eggs)
50 grams granulated sugar
2 drops green gel food coloring
1 recipe Pistachio Buttercream (page 188)

1. In a food processor, pulse the 2 grams of pistachios until finely ground.

2. Sift the 2 grams ground pistachios from the processor, almond flour, powdered sugar, and salt into a small to medium bowl. Set aside.

3. In another small to medium bowl, with an electric mixer on medium-high speed, beat the egg whites for 1 to 2 minutes until frothy. While beating on medium-high speed, slowly add the granulated sugar, then beat on high speed for about 3 minutes until the mixture is thicker and white. Add the food coloring and beat for 3 to 4 minutes until the meringue is thick, with firm, glossy peaks when you lift the beaters. Turn the bowl upside down; if the meringue does not move, it is ready. If not, whip in 1- to 2-minute increments until stiff peaks form.

4. With a silicone spatula, fold one-third of the almond flour mixture into the meringue until just combined. In two batches, fold in the remaining almond flour mixture. The batter should flow off the spatula, slowly but continuously, in unbroken ribbons.

5. Line a 13-by-18-inch baking sheet with a silicone macaron baking mat or parchment paper.

6. Transfer the batter to a pastry bag fitted with a Wilton #12 round tip. Pipe 24 to 30 (1½-inch) circles onto the prepared baking sheet, 1 to 1½ inches apart. Gently drop the baking sheet on the counter to eliminate air bubbles and level the macarons. Sprinkle the remaining 6 grams of finely ground pistachios evenly over the macarons (try not to put too much on any one shell or the shell may crack when baked). Dry the macarons at room temperature for 30 minutes to 2 hours, uncovered, until dull, firm, not sticky, and dry to the touch.

7. When the macarons look almost ready, position a rack in the center of the oven and preheat the oven to 300°F.

8. Bake the macarons on the center rack for 12 to 14 minutes, or until a macaron tapped on top moves only slightly.

9. Let cool for 15 to 30 minutes on a wire rack, then transfer the macarons to another tray to match similar-size shells.

10. Fill as directed in the filling recipe. Top each filled shell with another shell, then press and twist the shells together.

11. Remove from the refrigerator 30 minutes before serving.

CHANGE IT UP: Fill with Rose Buttercream (page 180), Salted Caramel Buttercream (page 178), or Toffee Filling (page 192).

EARL GREY MACARONS

PREP TIME: 30 minutes, plus 30 minutes to 2 hours to dry and 1 hour to refrigerate
BAKE TIME: 14 minutes
MAKES: 12 to 15 filled 1½-inch macarons

The distinctive flavor of black tea with bergamot creates a lovely taste experience when paired with a whipped white chocolate ganache. The vanilla macaron used here fits in perfectly with the tea-flavored filling. I prefer to color the shells a blue-gray hue to match the cornflowers found in the tea.

70 grams almond flour
50 grams powdered sugar
Pinch salt
53 grams egg whites (from about 2 medium eggs)
50 grams granulated sugar
1 gram (¼ teaspoon) vanilla extract
1 drop blue gel food coloring
1 drop black gel food coloring
1 recipe Tea Whipped White Chocolate Ganache (page 195), made with Earl Grey tea

1. Sift the almond flour, powdered sugar, and salt into a small to medium bowl. Set aside.

2. In another small to medium bowl, with an electric mixer on medium-high speed, beat the egg whites for 1 to 2 minutes until frothy. While beating on medium-high speed, slowly add the granulated sugar, then beat on high speed for about 3 minutes until the mixture is thicker and white. Add the vanilla and food colorings and beat for 3 to 4 minutes until the meringue is thick, with firm, glossy peaks when you lift the beaters. Turn the bowl upside down; if the meringue does not move, it is ready. If not, whip in 1- to 2-minute increments until stiff peaks form.

3. With a silicone spatula, fold one-third of the almond flour mixture into the meringue until just combined. In two batches, fold in the remaining almond flour mixture. The batter should flow off the spatula, slowly but continuously, in unbroken ribbons.

4. Line a 13-by-18-inch baking sheet with a silicone macaron baking mat or parchment paper.

5. Transfer the batter to a pastry bag fitted with a Wilton #12 round tip. Pipe 24 to 30 (1½-inch) circles onto the prepared baking sheet, 1 to 1½ inches apart. Gently drop the baking sheet on the counter to eliminate air bubbles and level the macarons. Dry the macarons at room temperature for 30 minutes to 2 hours, uncovered, until dull, firm, not sticky, and dry to the touch.

6. When the macarons look almost ready, position a rack in the center of the oven and preheat the oven to 300°F.

7. Bake the macarons on the center rack for 12 to 14 minutes, or until a macaron tapped on top moves only slightly.

8. Let cool for 15 to 30 minutes on a wire rack, then transfer the macarons to another tray to match similar-size shells.

9. Fill as directed in the filling recipe. Top each filled shell with another shell, then press and twist the shells together.

10. Remove from the refrigerator 30 minutes before serving.

CHANGE IT UP: Fill with Honey Lavender Whipped White Chocolate Ganache (page 196), Pistachio Buttercream (page 188), or Rose Buttercream (page 180).

MATCHA GREEN TEA MACARONS

PREP TIME: 30 minutes, plus 30 minutes to 2 hours to dry and 1 hour to refrigerate
BAKE TIME: 14 minutes
MAKES: 12 to 15 filled 1½-inch macarons

Matcha is one of my all-time favorite flavors. The earthiness of the green tea makes it a winning combination with the lightly sweet macaron shell, somewhat reminiscent of a matcha latte. For the best taste, use a culinary-grade matcha, like Matcha Love or Jade Leaf brand.

70 grams almond flour

48 grams powdered sugar

2 grams culinary-grade matcha powder

Pinch salt

53 grams egg whites (from about 2 medium eggs)

50 grams granulated sugar

1 or 2 drops green gel food coloring

1 recipe Matcha Buttercream (page 179)

1. Sift the almond flour, powdered sugar, matcha powder, and salt into a small to medium bowl. Set aside.

2. In another small to medium bowl, with an electric mixer on medium-high speed, beat the egg whites for 1 to 2 minutes until frothy. While beating on medium-high speed, slowly add the granulated sugar, then beat on high speed for about 3 minutes until the mixture is thicker and white. Add the food coloring and beat for 3 to 4 minutes until the meringue is thick, with firm, glossy peaks when you lift the beaters. Turn the bowl upside down; if the meringue does not move, it is ready. If not, whip in 1- to 2-minute increments until stiff peaks form.

3. With a silicone spatula, fold one-third of the almond flour mixture into the meringue until just combined. In two batches, fold in the remaining almond flour mixture. The batter should flow off the spatula, slowly but continuously, in unbroken ribbons.

4. Line a 13-by-18-inch baking sheet with a silicone macaron baking mat or parchment paper.

5. Transfer the batter to a pastry bag fitted with a Wilton #12 round tip. Pipe 24 to 30 (1½-inch) circles onto the prepared baking sheet, 1 to 1½ inches apart. Gently drop the baking sheet on the counter to eliminate air bubbles and level the macarons. Dry the macarons at room temperature for 30 minutes to 2 hours, uncovered, until dull, firm, not sticky, and dry to the touch.

6. When the macarons look almost ready, position a rack in the center of the oven and preheat the oven to 300°F.

7. Bake the macarons on the center rack for 12 to 14 minutes, or until a macaron tapped on top moves only slightly.

8. Let cool for 15 to 30 minutes on a wire rack, then transfer the macarons to another tray to match similar-size shells.

9. Fill as directed in the filling recipe. Top each filled shell with another shell, then press and twist the shells together.

10. Remove from the refrigerator 30 minutes before serving.

CHANGE IT UP: Fill with Strawberry Buttercream (page 166), Vanilla Buttercream (page 164), or Black Sesame Buttercream (page 181).

HONEY LAVENDER MACARONS

PREP TIME: 30 minutes, plus 30 minutes to 2 hours to dry and 1 hour to refrigerate
BAKE TIME: 14 minutes
MAKES: 12 to 15 filled 1½-inch macarons

Lavender is a sophisticated flavor, and honey gives it depth. When you taste these macarons, you'll be transported to a fresh lavender field. I prefer not to put lavender flowers in the shells because it can be too strong of a flavor for some people. These delightful macarons are a staple in French bakeries, like Rose Macarons (page 52). *Bon appétit!*

70 grams almond flour

50 grams powdered sugar

Pinch salt

53 grams egg whites (from about 2 medium eggs)

50 grams granulated sugar

1 gram (¼ teaspoon) vanilla extract

1 or 2 drops purple gel food coloring

1 recipe Honey Lavender Whipped White Chocolate Ganache (page 196)

1. Sift the almond flour, powdered sugar, and salt into a small to medium bowl. Set aside.

2. In another small to medium bowl, with an electric mixer on medium-high speed, beat the egg whites for 1 to 2 minutes until frothy. While beating on medium-high speed, slowly add the granulated sugar, then beat on high speed for about 3 minutes until the mixture is thicker and white, Add the vanilla and food coloring and beat for 3 to 4 minutes until the meringue is thick, with firm, glossy peaks when you lift the beaters. Turn the bowl upside down; if the meringue does not move, it is ready. If not, whip in 1- to 2-minute increments until stiff peaks form.

3. With a silicone spatula, fold one-third of the almond flour mixture into the meringue until just combined. In two batches, fold in the remaining almond flour mixture. The batter should flow off the spatula, slowly but continuously, in unbroken ribbons.

4. Line a 13-by-18-inch baking sheet with a silicone macaron baking mat or parchment paper.

5. Transfer the batter to a pastry bag fitted with a Wilton #12 round tip. Pipe 24 to 30 (1½-inch) circles onto the prepared baking sheet, 1 to 1½ inches apart. Gently drop the baking sheet on the counter to eliminate air bubbles and level the macarons. Dry the macarons at room temperature for 30 minutes to 2 hours, uncovered, until dull, firm, not sticky, and dry to the touch.

6. When the macarons look almost ready, position a rack in the center of the oven and preheat the oven to 300°F.

7. Bake the macarons on the center rack for 12 to 14 minutes, or until a macaron tapped on top moves only slightly.

8. Let cool for 15 to 30 minutes on a wire rack, then transfer the macarons to another tray to match similar-size shells.

9. Fill as directed in the filling recipe. Top each filled shell with another shell, then press and twist the shells together.

10. Remove from the refrigerator 30 minutes before serving.

CHANGE IT UP: Fill with Lemon Buttercream (page 167), Rose Buttercream (page 180), or White Chocolate Ganache (with White Chocolate Raspberry variation; page 197).

ROSE MACARONS

PREP TIME: 30 minutes, plus 30 minutes to 2 hours drying time
BAKE TIME: 14 minutes
MAKES: 12 to 15 filled 1½-inch macarons

Rose macarons are an essential in Parisian pâtisseries; the floral, sophisticated flavor of the flower elevates your palate. Floral macarons aren't for everyone, but rose is not overwhelming. When I eat these, it reminds me of a lush rose garden in France.

70 grams almond flour

50 grams powdered sugar

Pinch salt

53 grams egg whites (from about 2 medium eggs)

50 grams granulated sugar

1 gram (¼ teaspoon) rose water

1 drop pink gel food coloring

1 recipe Rose Buttercream (page 180)

1. Sift the almond flour, powdered sugar, and salt into a small to medium bowl. Set aside.

2. In another small to medium bowl, with an electric mixer on medium-high speed, beat the egg whites for 1 to 2 minutes until frothy. While beating on medium-high speed, slowly add the granulated sugar, then beat on high speed for about 3 minutes until the mixture is thicker and white. Add the rose water and food coloring and beat for 3 to 4 minutes until the meringue is thick, with firm, glossy peaks when you lift the beaters. Turn the bowl upside down; if the meringue does not move, it is ready. If not, whip in 1- to 2-minute increments until stiff peaks form.

3. With a silicone spatula, fold one-third of the almond flour mixture into the meringue until just combined. In two batches, fold in the remaining almond flour mixture. The batter should flow off the spatula, slowly but continuously, in unbroken ribbons.

4. Line a 13-by-18-inch baking sheet with a silicone macaron baking mat or parchment paper.

5. Transfer the batter to a pastry bag fitted with a Wilton #12 round tip. Pipe 24 to 30 (1½-inch) circles onto the prepared baking sheet, 1 to 1½ inches apart. Gently drop the baking sheet on the counter to eliminate air bubbles and level the macarons. Dry the macarons at room temperature for 30 minutes to 2 hours, uncovered, until dull, firm, not sticky, and dry to the touch.

6. When the macarons look almost ready, position a rack in the center of the oven and preheat the oven to 300°F.

7. Bake the macarons on the center rack for 12 to 14 minutes, or until a macaron tapped on top moves only slightly.

8. Let cool for 15 to 30 minutes on a wire rack, then transfer the macarons to another tray to match similar-size shells.

9. Fill as directed in the filling recipe. Top each filled shell with another shell, then press and twist the shells together.

10. Remove from the refrigerator 30 minutes before serving.

CHANGE IT UP: Fill with Lemon Buttercream (page 167), Pistachio Buttercream (page 188), or Toasted Almond Buttercream (page 189).

RED VELVET MACARONS

PREP TIME: 30 minutes, plus 30 minutes to 2 hours to dry and 1 hour to refrigerate
BAKE TIME: 14 minutes
MAKES: 12 to 15 filled 1½-inch macarons

Did you know that red velvet cake was created during World War II when supplies, such as cocoa powder, were rationed? Bakers used red beet juice to hide the fact that the cake had less cocoa than the usual chocolate cake. Today, red velvet stands on its own, and it tastes delicious as a macaron as well!

70 grams almond flour

45 grams powdered sugar

5 grams unsweetened
cocoa powder

Pinch salt

53 grams egg whites (from
about 2 medium eggs)

50 grams granulated sugar

4 or 5 drops red gel food
coloring

1 recipe Cream Cheese
Buttercream (page 176)

1. Sift the almond flour, powdered sugar, cocoa powder, and salt into a small to medium bowl. Set aside.

2. In another small to medium bowl, with an electric mixer on medium-high speed, beat the egg whites for 1 to 2 minutes until frothy. While beating on medium-high speed, slowly add the granulated sugar, then beat on high speed for about 3 minutes until the mixture is thicker and white. Add the food coloring and beat for 3 to 4 minutes until the meringue is thick, with firm, glossy peaks when you lift the beaters. Turn the bowl upside down; if the meringue does not move, it is ready. If not, whip in 1- to 2-minute increments until stiff peaks form.

3. With a silicone spatula, fold one-third of the almond flour mixture into the meringue until just combined. In two batches, fold in the remaining almond flour mixture. The batter should flow off the spatula, slowly but continuously, in unbroken ribbons.

4. Line a 13-by-18-inch baking sheet with a silicone macaron baking mat or parchment paper.

5. Transfer the batter to a pastry bag fitted with a Wilton #12 round tip. Pipe 24 to 30 (1½-inch) circles onto the prepared baking sheet, 1 to 1½ inches apart. Gently drop the baking sheet on the counter to eliminate air bubbles and level the macarons. Dry the macarons at room temperature for 30 minutes to 2 hours, uncovered, until dull, firm, not sticky, and dry to the touch.

6. When the macarons look almost ready, position a rack in the center of the oven and preheat the oven to 300°F.

7. Bake the macarons on the center rack for 12 to 14 minutes, or until a macaron tapped on top moves only slightly.

8. Let cool for 15 to 30 minutes on a wire rack, then transfer the macarons to another tray to match similar-size shells.

9. Fill as directed in the filling recipe. Top each filled shell with another shell, then press and twist the shells together.

10. Remove from the refrigerator 30 minutes before serving.

CHANGE IT UP: Fill with Chocolate Buttercream (page 165), Cookies and Cream Buttercream (page 175), or Hazelnut Chocolate Buttercream (page 190).

MOCHA MACARONS

PREP TIME: 30 minutes, plus 30 minutes to 2 hours to dry and 1 hour to refrigerate
BAKE TIME: 14 minutes
MAKES: 12 to 15 filled 1½-inch macarons

Mocha is a classic flavor that reminds me of the coffee shop, with its delicious chocolate flavor combined with roasted coffee. These treats give you both the jump-start of coffee and the richness of chocolate. What could be better?

70 grams almond flour

45 grams powdered sugar

5 grams unsweetened cocoa powder

1 gram (¼ teaspoon) instant coffee

Pinch salt

53 grams egg whites (from about 2 medium eggs)

50 grams granulated sugar

2 drops brown gel food coloring

1 tablespoon ground coffee (optional)

1 recipe Mocha Ganache (page 193)

1. Sift the almond flour, powdered sugar, cocoa powder, instant coffee, and salt into a small to medium bowl. Set aside.

2. In another small to medium bowl, with an electric mixer on medium-high speed, beat the egg whites for 1 to 2 minutes until frothy. While beating on medium-high speed, slowly add the granulated sugar, then beat on high speed for about 3 minutes until the mixture is thicker and white. Add the food coloring and beat for 3 to 4 minutes until the meringue is thick, with firm, glossy peaks when you lift the beaters. Turn the bowl upside down; if the meringue does not move, it is ready. If not, whip in 1- to 2-minute increments until stiff peaks form.

3. With a silicone spatula, fold one-third of the almond flour mixture into the meringue until just combined. In two batches, fold in the remaining almond flour mixture. The batter should flow off the spatula, slowly but continuously, in unbroken ribbons.

4. Line a 13-by-18-inch baking sheet with a silicone macaron baking mat or parchment paper.

5. Transfer the batter to a pastry bag fitted with a Wilton #12 round tip. Pipe 24 to 30 (1½-inch) circles onto the prepared baking sheet, 1 to 1½ inches apart. Gently drop the baking sheet on the counter to eliminate air bubbles and level the macarons. Sprinkle the tops with ground coffee (if using). Dry the macarons at room temperature for 30 minutes to 2 hours, uncovered, until dull, firm, not sticky, and dry to the touch.

6. When the macarons look almost ready, position a rack in the center of the oven and preheat the oven to 300°F.

7. Bake the macarons on the center rack for 12 to 14 minutes, or until a macaron tapped on top moves only slightly.

8. Let cool for 15 to 30 minutes on a wire rack, then transfer the macarons to another tray to match similar-size shells.

9. Fill as directed in the filling recipe. Top each filled shell with another shell, then press and twist the shells together.

10. Remove from the refrigerator 30 minutes before serving.

CHANGE IT UP: Fill with Chocolate Buttercream (page 165), Cookies and Cream Buttercream (page 175), or Toffee Filling (page 192).

ESPRESSO MACARONS

PREP TIME: 30 minutes, plus 30 minutes to 2 hours to dry and 1 hour to refrigerate
BAKE TIME: 14 minutes
MAKES: 12 to 15 filled 1½-inch macarons

These macarons are inspired by freshly brewed coffee and will definitely kick-start your day! The roasted coffee flavor goes perfectly with the smooth espresso buttercream. Any coffee lover would enjoy these not-too-sweet macarons, which are perfect to share at the office.

70 grams almond flour

50 grams powdered sugar

1 gram (¼ teaspoon) instant coffee

Pinch salt

53 grams egg whites (from about 2 medium eggs)

50 grams granulated sugar

1 drop brown gel food coloring

1 recipe Espresso Buttercream (page 183)

1. Sift the almond flour, powdered sugar, instant coffee, and salt into a small to medium bowl. Set aside.

2. In another small to medium bowl, with an electric mixer on medium-high speed, beat the egg whites for 1 to 2 minutes until frothy. While beating on medium-high speed, slowly add the granulated sugar, then beat on high speed for about 3 minutes until the mixture is thicker and white. Add the food coloring and beat for 3 to 4 minutes until the meringue is thick, with firm, glossy peaks when you lift the beaters. Turn the bowl upside down; if the meringue does not move, it is ready. If not, whip in 1- to 2-minute increments until stiff peaks form.

3. With a silicone spatula, fold one-third of the almond flour mixture into the meringue until just combined. In two batches, fold in the remaining almond flour mixture. The batter should flow off the spatula, slowly but continuously, in unbroken ribbons.

4. Line a 13-by-18-inch baking sheet with a silicone macaron baking mat or parchment paper.

5. Transfer the batter to a pastry bag fitted with a Wilton #12 round tip. Pipe 24 to 30 (1½-inch) circles onto the prepared baking sheet, 1 to 1½ inches apart. Gently drop the baking sheet on the counter to eliminate air bubbles and level the macarons. Dry the macarons at room temperature for 30 minutes to 2 hours, uncovered, until dull, firm, not sticky, and dry to the touch.

6. When the macarons look almost ready, position a rack in the center of the oven and preheat the oven to 300°F.

7. Bake the macarons on the center rack for 12 to 14 minutes, or until a macaron tapped on top moves only slightly.

8. Let cool for 15 to 30 minutes on a wire rack, then transfer the macarons to another tray to match similar-size shells.

9. Fill as directed in the filling recipe. Top each filled shell with another shell, then press and twist the shells together.

10. Remove from the refrigerator 30 minutes before serving.

CHANGE IT UP: Fill with Chocolate Buttercream (page 165), Salted Caramel Buttercream (page 178), or Mocha Ganache (page 193).

SALTED CARAMEL MACARONS

PREP TIME: 30 minutes, plus 30 minutes to 2 hours to dry and 1 hour to refrigerate

BAKE TIME: 14 minutes

MAKES: 12 to 15 filled 1½-inch macarons

This buttery, rich, creamy macaron will have you swooning, especially if you are a caramel fan. The vanilla macaron shell pairs nicely with the star of the show, the salted caramel buttercream. The sea salt in the buttercream filling offsets the sweetness of the caramel.

70 grams almond flour

50 grams powdered sugar

Pinch salt

53 grams egg whites (from about 2 medium eggs)

50 grams granulated sugar

1 gram (¼ teaspoon) vanilla extract

1 drop brown gel food coloring

1 recipe Salted Caramel Buttercream (page 178)

1. Sift the almond flour, powdered sugar, and salt into a small to medium bowl. Set aside.

2. In another small to medium bowl, with an electric mixer on medium-high speed, beat the egg whites for 1 to 2 minutes until frothy. While beating on medium-high speed, slowly add the granulated sugar, then beat on high speed for about 3 minutes until the mixture is thicker and white. Add the vanilla and food coloring and beat for 3 to 4 minutes until the meringue is thick, with firm, glossy peaks when you lift the beaters. Turn the bowl upside down; if the meringue does not move, it is ready. If not, whip in 1- to 2-minute increments until stiff peaks form.

3. With a silicone spatula, fold one-third of the almond flour mixture into the meringue until just combined. In two batches, fold in the remaining almond flour mixture. The batter should flow off the spatula, slowly but continuously, in unbroken ribbons.

4. Line a 13-by-18-inch baking sheet with a silicone macaron baking mat or parchment paper.

5. Transfer the batter to a pastry bag fitted with a Wilton #12 round tip. Pipe 24 to 30 (1½-inch) circles onto the prepared baking sheet, 1 to 1½ inches apart. Gently drop the baking sheet on the counter to eliminate air bubbles and level the macarons. Dry the macarons at room temperature for 30 minutes to 2 hours, uncovered, until dull, firm, not sticky, and dry to the touch.

6. When the macarons look almost ready, position a rack in the center of the oven and preheat the oven to 300°F.

7. Bake the macarons on the center rack for 12 to 14 minutes, or until a macaron tapped on top moves only slightly.

8. Let cool for 15 to 30 minutes on a wire rack, then transfer the macarons to another tray to match similar-size shells.

9. Fill as directed in the filling recipe. Top each filled shell with another shell, then press and twist the shells together.

10. Remove from the refrigerator 30 minutes before serving.

CHANGE IT UP: Fill with Chocolate Buttercream (page 165), Mocha Ganache (page 193), or Cookie Butter Buttercream (page 174).

TIRAMISU MACARONS

PREP TIME: 30 minutes, plus 30 minutes to 2 hours to dry and 1 hour to refrigerate
BAKE TIME: 14 minutes
MAKES: 12 to 15 filled 1½-inch macarons

Tiramisu is one of my favorite desserts (other than macarons!) because it is lightly sweetened, infused with fresh cream and coffee, and topped with cocoa powder. I love these flavors so much that I turned them into a macaron. I don't use mascarpone buttercream for the filling because it's more difficult to make than regular vanilla buttercream, but you get the same flavors.

70 grams almond flour
50 grams powdered sugar
1 gram (¼ teaspoon) instant coffee
Pinch salt
53 grams egg whites (from about 2 medium eggs)
50 grams granulated sugar
1½ teaspoons unsweetened cocoa powder
1 recipe Vanilla Buttercream (page 164)

1. Sift the almond flour, powdered sugar, instant coffee, and salt into a small to medium bowl. Set aside.

2. In another small to medium bowl, with an electric mixer on medium-high speed, beat the egg whites for 1 to 2 minutes until frothy. While beating on medium-high speed, slowly add the granulated sugar, then beat on high speed for 6 to 7 minutes until the meringue is white and thick, with firm, glossy peaks when you lift the beaters. Turn the bowl upside down; if the meringue does not move, it is ready. If not, whip in 1- to 2-minute increments until stiff peaks form.

3. With a silicone spatula, fold one-third of the almond flour mixture into the meringue until just combined. In two batches, fold in the remaining almond flour mixture. The batter should flow off the spatula, slowly but continuously, in unbroken ribbons.

4. Line a 13-by-18-inch baking sheet with a silicone macaron baking mat or parchment paper.

5. Transfer the batter to a pastry bag fitted with a Wilton #12 round tip. Pipe 24 to 30 (1½-inch) circles onto the prepared baking sheet, 1 to 1½ inches apart. Gently drop the baking sheet on the counter to eliminate air bubbles and level the macarons. Use a fine-mesh strainer to dust the cocoa powder over the tops of the macaron shells. Dry the macarons at room temperature for 30 minutes to 2 hours, uncovered, until dull, firm, not sticky, and dry to the touch.

6. When the macarons look almost ready, position a rack in the center of the oven and preheat the oven to 300°F.

7. Bake the macarons on the center rack for 12 to 14 minutes, or until a macaron tapped on top moves only slightly.

8. Let cool for 15 to 30 minutes on a wire rack, then transfer the macarons to another tray to match similar-size shells.

9. Fill as directed in the filling recipe. Top each filled shell with another shell, then press and twist the shells together.

10. Remove from the refrigerator 30 minutes before serving.

CHANGE IT UP: Fill with Chocolate Buttercream (page 165), Hazelnut Chocolate Buttercream (page 190), or Toffee Filling (page 192).

Pandan Coconut Macarons page 84

CHAPTER 3

New Creations

Fruity Cereal Macarons 66

Crunchy Cinnamon Cereal Macarons 68

Cookie Butter Macarons 70

Cookies and Cream Macarons 72

Black Sesame Macarons 74

Dark-Roast Oolong Tea Macarons 76

Thai Tea Macarons 78

Jasmine Milk Tea Macarons 80

Blueberry Matcha
Latte Macarons 82

Pandan Coconut Macarons 84

Pineapple Coconut Macarons 86

Passion Fruit Guava Macarons 88

Raspberry Cheesecake Macarons 90

Strawberry Shortcake Macarons 92

Carrot Cake Macarons 94

Crème Brûlée Macarons 96

Chocolate Banana Macarons 98

Hazelnut Chocolate Macarons 100

White Chocolate
Macadamia Macarons 102

White Rabbit Candy Macarons 104

FRUITY CEREAL MACARONS

PREP TIME: 30 minutes, plus 30 minutes to 2 hours to dry and 1 hour to refrigerate
BAKE TIME: 14 minutes
MAKES: 12 to 15 filled 1½-inch macarons

Fruity cereal macarons are one of my customers' favorite flavors because it reminds them of childhood. There's cereal in the shell and buttercream, but you can also sprinkle the shells with more fruity cereal as a garnish. Choose festive colors for your shells, like purple, blue, or pink.

5 grams fruity cereal, plus
   1½ teaspoons
70 grams almond flour
45 grams powdered sugar
Pinch salt
53 grams egg whites (from
   about 2 medium eggs)
50 grams granulated sugar
2 drops purple, blue, or pink
   gel food coloring
1 recipe Fruity Cereal
   Buttercream (page 172)

1. In a food processor, pulse the 5 grams of fruity cereal into a powder.

2. Sift the almond flour, powdered sugar, cereal powder, and salt into a small to medium bowl. Set aside.

3. In another small to medium bowl, with an electric mixer on medium-high speed, beat the egg whites for 1 to 2 minutes until frothy. While beating on medium-high speed, slowly add the granulated sugar, then beat on high speed for about 3 minutes until the mixture is thicker and white. Add the food coloring and beat for 3 to 4 minutes until the meringue is thick, with firm, glossy peaks when you lift the beaters. Turn the bowl upside down; if the meringue does not move, it is ready. If not, whip in 1- to 2-minute increments until stiff peaks form.

4. With a silicone spatula, fold one-third of the almond flour mixture into the meringue until just combined. In two batches, fold in the remaining almond flour mixture. The batter should flow off the spatula, slowly but continuously, in unbroken ribbons.

5. Line a 13-by-18-inch baking sheet with a silicone macaron baking mat or parchment paper.

6. Transfer the batter to a pastry bag fitted with a Wilton #12 round tip. Pipe 24 to 30 (1½-inch) circles onto the prepared baking sheet, 1 to 1½ inches apart. Gently drop the baking sheet on the counter to eliminate air bubbles and level the macarons. Lightly sprinkle the macarons with the remaining 1½ teaspoons of cereal. Dry the macarons at room temperature for 30 minutes to 2 hours, uncovered, until dull, firm, not sticky, and dry to the touch.

7. When the macarons look almost ready, position a rack in the center of the oven and preheat the oven to 300°F.

8. Bake the macarons on the center rack for 12 to 14 minutes, or until a macaron tapped on top moves only slightly.

9. Let cool for 15 to 30 minutes on a wire rack, then transfer the macarons to another tray to match similar-size shells.

10. Fill as directed in the filling recipe. Top each filled shell with another shell, then press and twist the shells together.

11. Remove from the refrigerator 30 minutes before serving.

CHANGE IT UP: Fill with Strawberry Buttercream (page 166), Vanilla Buttercream (page 164), or Mango Buttercream (page 168).

CRUNCHY CINNAMON CEREAL MACARONS

PREP TIME: 30 minutes, plus 30 minutes to 2 hours to dry and 1 hour to refrigerate
BAKE TIME: 14 minutes
MAKES: 12 to 15 filled 1½-inch macarons

One of my favorite cereals is Cinnamon Toast Crunch because of its sugary sweet flavor, especially when it mixes with milk. I decided that turning this flavor into a macaron would be delicious—and it is! With a chewy macaron shell, it makes a wonderful textural experience, too.

70 grams almond flour

50 grams powdered sugar

1 gram ground cinnamon

Pinch salt

53 grams egg whites (from about 2 medium eggs)

50 grams granulated sugar

1 drop brown gel food coloring

15 pieces Cinnamon Toast Crunch cereal

1 recipe Cinnamon Buttercream (page 173)

1. Sift the almond flour, powdered sugar, cinnamon, and salt into a small to medium bowl. Set aside.

2. In another small to medium bowl, with an electric mixer on medium-high speed, beat the egg whites for 1 to 2 minutes until frothy. While beating on medium-high speed, slowly add the granulated sugar, then beat on high speed for about 3 minutes until the mixture is thicker and white. Add the food coloring and beat for 3 to 4 minutes until the meringue is thick, with firm, glossy peaks when you lift the beaters. Turn the bowl upside down; if the meringue does not move, it is ready. If not, whip in 1- to 2-minute increments until stiff peaks form.

3. With a silicone spatula, fold one-third of the almond flour mixture into the meringue until just combined. In two batches, fold in the remaining almond flour mixture. The batter should flow off the spatula, slowly but continuously, in unbroken ribbons.

4. Line a 13-by-18-inch baking sheet with a silicone macaron baking mat or parchment paper.

5. Transfer the batter to a pastry bag fitted with a Wilton #12 round tip. Pipe 24 to 30 (1½-inch) circles onto the prepared baking sheet, 1 to 1½ inches apart. Gently drop the baking sheet on the counter to eliminate air bubbles and level the macarons. Dry the macarons at room temperature for 30 minutes to 2 hours, uncovered, until dull, firm, not sticky, and dry to the touch.

6. When the macarons look almost ready, position a rack in the center of the oven and preheat the oven to 300°F.

7. Bake the macarons on the center rack for 12 to 14 minutes, or until a macaron tapped on top moves only slightly.

8. Let cool for 15 to 30 minutes on a wire rack, then transfer the macarons to another tray to match similar-size shells.

9. Fill as directed in the filling recipe. Place a piece of cereal on the filling in the center of the shell. Top each filled shell with another shell, then press and twist the shells together. Refrigerate for at least 1 hour, or overnight.

10. Remove from the refrigerator 30 minutes before serving.

CHANGE IT UP: Fill with Toasted Almond Buttercream (page 189), Salted Caramel Buttercream (page 178), or Vanilla Buttercream (page 164).

COOKIE BUTTER MACARONS

PREP TIME: 30 minutes, plus 30 minutes to 2 hours to dry and 1 hour to refrigerate
BAKE TIME: 14 minutes
MAKES: 12 to 15 filled 1½-inch macarons

Have you tried cookie butter? It's a delicious gingerbread-like spread sold at many grocery stores. It reminds me of Christmas, warm blankets, and happy times. If not, you're in for a treat. Now, you can get the texture of a macaron with the yummy taste of cookie butter, which will make your taste buds sing!

70 grams almond flour
50 grams powdered sugar
Pinch salt
53 grams egg whites (from about 2 medium eggs)
50 grams granulated sugar
1½ teaspoons finely chopped shortbread cookies (such as Biscoff)
1 recipe Cookie Butter Buttercream (page 174)

1. Sift the almond flour, powdered sugar, and salt into a small to medium bowl. Set aside.

2. In another small to medium bowl, with an electric mixer on medium-high speed, beat the egg whites for 1 to 2 minutes until frothy. While beating on medium-high speed, slowly add the granulated sugar, then beat on high speed for 6 to 7 minutes until the meringue is white and thick, with firm, glossy peaks when you lift the beaters. Turn the bowl upside down; if the meringue does not move, it is ready. If not, whip in 1- to 2-minute increments until stiff peaks form.

3. With a silicone spatula, fold one-third of the almond flour mixture into the meringue until just combined. In two batches, fold in the remaining almond flour mixture. The batter should flow off the spatula, slowly but continuously, in unbroken ribbons.

4. Line a 13-by-18-inch baking sheet with a silicone macaron baking mat or parchment paper.

5. Transfer the batter to a pastry bag fitted with a Wilton #12 round tip. Pipe 24 to 30 (1½-inch) circles onto the prepared baking sheet, 1 to 1½ inches apart. Gently drop the baking sheet on the counter to eliminate air bubbles and level the macarons. Sprinkle the cookie crumbs on top of the macarons. Dry the macarons at room temperature for 30 minutes to 2 hours, uncovered, until dull, firm, not sticky, and dry to the touch.

6. When the macarons look almost ready, position a rack in the center of the oven and preheat the oven to 300°F.

7. Bake the macarons on the center rack for 12 to 14 minutes, or until a macaron tapped on top moves only slightly.

8. Let cool for 15 to 30 minutes on a wire rack, then transfer the macarons to another tray to match similar-size shells.

9. Fill as directed in the filling recipe. Top each filled shell with another shell, then press and twist the shells together.

10. Remove from the refrigerator 30 minutes before serving.

CHANGE IT UP: Fill with Cinnamon Buttercream (page 173), Chocolate Buttercream (page 165), or Toffee Filling (page 192).

COOKIES AND CREAM MACARONS

PREP TIME: 30 minutes, plus 30 minutes to 2 hours to dry and 1 hour to refrigerate

BAKE TIME: 14 minutes

MAKES: 12 to 15 filled 1½-inch macarons

Who doesn't love Oreos? These macarons are one of my most popular flavors. They have a strong Oreo flavor, similar to eating cookies and ice cream. Sprinkling crushed Oreos on top and putting them in the shell really makes the texture pop.

5 grams Oreos, plus 1½ teaspoons finely chopped

70 grams almond flour

45 grams powdered sugar

Pinch salt

53 grams egg whites (from about 2 medium eggs)

50 grams granulated sugar

1 drop black gel food coloring

1 recipe Cookies and Cream Buttercream (page 175)

1. In a food processor, pulse the 5 grams of Oreos into a powder.

2. Sift the almond flour, powdered sugar, Oreo powder, and salt into a small to medium bowl. Set aside.

3. In another small to medium bowl, with an electric mixer on medium-high speed, beat the egg whites for 1 to 2 minutes until frothy. While beating on medium-high speed, slowly add the granulated sugar, then beat on high speed for about 3 minutes until the mixture is thicker and white. Add the food coloring and beat for 3 to 4 minutes until the meringue is thick, with firm, glossy peaks when you lift the beaters. Turn the bowl upside down; if the meringue does not move, it is ready. If not, whip in 1- to 2-minute increments until stiff peaks form.

4. With a silicone spatula, fold one-third of the almond flour mixture into the meringue until just combined. In two batches, fold in the remaining almond flour mixture. The batter should flow off the spatula, slowly but continuously, in unbroken ribbons.

5. Line a 13-by-18-inch baking sheet with a silicone macaron baking mat or parchment paper.

6. Transfer the batter to a pastry bag fitted with a Wilton #12 round tip. Pipe 24 to 30 (1½-inch) circles onto the prepared baking sheet, 1 to 1½ inches apart. Gently drop the baking sheet on the counter to eliminate air bubbles and level the macarons. Sprinkle the macarons with the chopped Oreos. Dry the macarons at room temperature for 30 minutes to 2 hours, uncovered, until dull, firm, not sticky, and dry to the touch.

7. When the macarons look almost ready, position a rack in the center of the oven and preheat the oven to 300°F.

8. Bake the macarons on the center rack for 12 to 14 minutes, or until a macaron tapped on top moves only slightly.

9. Let cool for 15 to 30 minutes on a wire rack, then transfer the macarons to another tray to match similar-size shells.

10. Fill as directed in the filling recipe. Top each filled shell with another shell, then press and twist the shells together.

11. Remove from the refrigerator 30 minutes before serving.

CHANGE IT UP: Fill with Matcha Buttercream (page 179), Cinnamon Buttercream (page 173), or Vanilla Buttercream (page 164).

BLACK SESAME MACARONS

PREP TIME: 30 minutes, plus 30 minutes to 2 hours to dry and 1 hour to refrigerate
BAKE TIME: 14 minutes
MAKES: 12 to 15 filled 1½-inch macarons

If you've never tried black sesame seeds, you're in for a treat. Black sesame has a nutty, earthy flavor that goes well with lightly sweet macarons. You can find black sesame powder at Asian markets. You can also grind the seeds in a food processor into a powder.

70 grams almond flour

45 grams powdered sugar

5 grams black
  sesame powder

Pinch salt

53 grams egg whites (from
  about 2 medium eggs)

50 grams granulated sugar

1 drop black gel food coloring

1½ teaspoons black
  sesame seeds

1 recipe Black Sesame
  Buttercream (page 181)

1. Sift the almond flour, powdered sugar, black sesame powder, and salt into a small to medium bowl. Set aside.

2. In another small to medium bowl, with an electric mixer on medium-high speed, beat the egg whites for 1 to 2 minutes until frothy. While beating on medium-high speed, slowly add the granulated sugar, then beat on high speed for about 3 minutes until the mixture is thicker and white. Add the food coloring and beat for 3 to 4 minutes until the meringue is thick, with firm, glossy peaks when you lift the beaters. Turn the bowl upside down; if the meringue does not move, it is ready. If not, whip in 1- to 2-minute increments until stiff peaks form.

3. With a silicone spatula, fold one-third of the almond flour mixture into the meringue until just combined. In two batches, fold in the remaining almond flour mixture. The batter should flow off the spatula, slowly but continuously, in unbroken ribbons.

4. Line a 13-by-18-inch baking sheet with a silicone macaron baking mat or parchment paper.

5. Transfer the batter to a pastry bag fitted with a Wilton #12 round tip. Pipe 24 to 30 (1½-inch) circles onto the prepared baking sheet, 1 to 1½ inches apart. Gently drop the baking sheet on the counter to eliminate air bubbles and level the macarons. Sprinkle the macarons with the black sesame seeds. Dry the macarons at room temperature for 30 minutes to 2 hours, uncovered, until dull, firm, not sticky, and dry to the touch.

6. When the macarons look almost ready, position a rack in the center of the oven and preheat the oven to 300°F.

7. Bake the macarons on the center rack for 12 to 14 minutes, or until a macaron tapped on top moves only slightly.

8. Let cool for 15 to 30 minutes on a wire rack, then transfer the macarons to another tray to match similar-size shells.

9. Fill as directed in the filling recipe. Top each filled shell with another shell, then press and twist the shells together.

10. Remove from the refrigerator 30 minutes before serving.

CHANGE IT UP: Fill with Matcha Buttercream (page 179), Chocolate Buttercream (page 165), or Pistachio Buttercream (page 188).

DARK-ROAST OOLONG TEA MACARONS

PREP TIME: 30 minutes, plus 30 minutes to 2 hours to dry and 1 hour to refrigerate
BAKE TIME: 14 minutes
MAKES: 12 to 15 filled 1½-inch macarons

This is one of my favorite types of tea when I go to bubble tea shops. Oolong has a pronounced, roasted flavor that truly sets it apart from the others. This flavor goes well with a vanilla macaron shell, and it looks especially pretty colored a light brown and brushed with edible gold paint.

70 grams almond flour

50 grams powdered sugar

Pinch salt

53 grams egg whites (from about 2 medium eggs)

50 grams granulated sugar

1 gram (¼ teaspoon) vanilla extract

1 drop brown gel food coloring

Edible gold paint, for decorating (optional)

1 recipe Tea Whipped White Chocolate Ganache (page 195), made with dark-roast oolong tea

1. Sift the almond flour, powdered sugar, and salt into a small to medium bowl. Set aside.

2. In another small to medium bowl, with an electric mixer on medium-high speed, beat the egg whites for 1 to 2 minutes until frothy. While beating on medium-high speed, slowly add the granulated sugar, then beat on high speed for about 3 minutes until the mixture is thicker and white. Add the vanilla and food coloring and beat for 3 to 4 minutes, until the meringue is thick, with firm, glossy peaks when you lift the beaters. Turn the bowl upside down; if the meringue does not move, it is ready. If not, whip in 1- to 2-minute increments until stiff peaks form.

3. With a silicone spatula, fold one-third of the almond flour mixture into the meringue until just combined. In two batches, fold in the remaining almond flour mixture. The batter should flow off the spatula, slowly but continuously, in unbroken ribbons.

4. Line a 13-by-18-inch baking sheet with a silicone macaron baking mat or parchment paper.

5. Transfer the batter to a pastry bag fitted with a Wilton #12 round tip. Pipe 24 to 30 (1½-inch) circles onto the prepared baking sheet, 1 inch apart. Gently drop the baking sheet on the counter to eliminate air bubbles and level the macarons. Dry the macarons at room temperature for 30 minutes to 2 hours, uncovered, until dull, firm, not sticky, and dry to the touch.

6. When the macarons look almost ready, position a rack in the center of the oven and preheat the oven to 300°F.

7. Bake the macarons on the center rack for 12 to 14 minutes, or until a macaron tapped on top moves only slightly.

8. Let cool for 15 to 30 minutes on a wire rack, then transfer the macarons to another tray to match similar-size shells.

9. Fill as directed in the filling recipe. Top each filled shell with another shell, then press and twist the shells together.

10. Use a food-safe paintbrush to brush the shells with the edible paint (if using). Refrigerate for at least 1 hour, or overnight.

11. Remove from the refrigerator 30 minutes before serving.

CHANGE IT UP: Fill with Tea Whipped White Chocolate Ganache (page 195) made with Earl Grey, jasmine, or Thai tea.

THAI TEA MACARONS

PREP TIME: 30 minutes, plus 30 minutes to 2 hours to dry and 1 hour to refrigerate
BAKE TIME: 14 minutes
MAKES: 12 to 15 filled 1½-inch macarons

Whenever I go to a Thai restaurant, I always get curry and a Thai tea to cool the spiciness. The sweetness and aromatic spices are a real treat, and the same is true in this macaron. The Thai tea–infused ganache, combined with an orange-tinted vanilla shell, looks and tastes like the popular drink.

70 grams almond flour

50 grams powdered sugar

Pinch salt

53 grams egg whites (from about 2 medium eggs)

50 grams granulated sugar

1 gram (¼ teaspoon) vanilla extract

2 drops orange gel food coloring

1½ teaspoons Thai tea leaves

1 recipe Tea Whipped White Chocolate Ganache (page 195), made with Thai tea

1. Sift the almond flour, powdered sugar, and salt into a small to medium bowl. Set aside.

2. In another small to medium bowl, with an electric mixer on medium-high speed, beat the egg whites for 1 to 2 minutes until frothy. While beating on medium-high speed, slowly add the granulated sugar, then beat on high speed for about 3 minutes until the mixture is thicker and white. Add the vanilla and food coloring and beat for 3 to 4 minutes until the meringue is thick, with firm, glossy peaks when you lift the beaters. Turn the bowl upside down; if the meringue does not move, it is ready. If not, whip in 1- to 2-minute increments until stiff peaks form.

3. With a silicone spatula, fold one-third of the almond flour mixture into the meringue until just combined. In two batches, fold in the remaining almond flour mixture. The batter should flow off the spatula, slowly but continuously, in unbroken ribbons.

4. Line a 13-by-18-inch baking sheet with a silicone macaron baking mat or parchment paper.

5. Transfer the batter to a pastry bag fitted with a Wilton #12 round tip. Pipe 24 to 30 (1½-inch) circles onto the prepared baking sheet, 1 to 1½ inches apart. Gently drop the baking sheet on the counter to eliminate air bubbles and level the macarons. Lightly sprinkle the macarons with the tea leaves. Dry the macarons at room temperature for 30 minutes to 2 hours, uncovered, until dull, firm, not sticky, and dry to the touch.

6. When the macarons look almost ready, position a rack in the center of the oven and preheat the oven to 300°F.

7. Bake the macarons on the center rack for 12 to 14 minutes, or until a macaron tapped on top moves only slightly.

8. Let cool for 15 to 30 minutes on a wire rack, then transfer the macarons to another tray to match similar-size shells.

9. Fill as directed in the filling recipe. Top each filled shell with another shell, then press and twist the shells together.

10. Remove from the refrigerator 30 minutes before serving.

CHANGE IT UP: Fill with Tea Whipped White Chocolate Ganache (page 195), made with jasmine or dark-roast oolong tea, or Honey Lavender Whipped White Chocolate Ganache (page 196).

JASMINE MILK TEA MACARONS

PREP TIME: 30 minutes, plus 30 minutes to 2 hours to dry and 1 hour to refrigerate

BAKE TIME: 14 minutes

MAKES: 12 to 15 filled 1½-inch macarons

When I first went to a bubble tea shop, I ordered jasmine milk tea, and I've been in love with it ever since! I *had* to make it into a macaron. The jasmine tea–infused ganache is divine!

70 grams almond flour

50 grams powdered sugar

Pinch salt

53 grams egg whites (from about 2 medium eggs),

50 grams granulated sugar

1 gram (¼ teaspoon) vanilla extract

2 drops blue gel food coloring

1 drop purple gel food coloring

1 recipe Tea Whipped White Chocolate Ganache (page 195), made with jasmine tea

1. Sift the almond flour, powdered sugar, and salt into a small to medium bowl. Set aside.

2. In another small to medium bowl, with an electric mixer on medium-high speed, beat the egg whites for 1 to 2 minutes until frothy. While beating on medium-high speed, slowly add the granulated sugar, then beat on high speed for about 3 minutes until the mixture is thicker and white. Add the vanilla and blue food coloring and beat for 3 to 4 minutes until the meringue is thick, with firm, glossy peaks when you lift the beaters. Turn the bowl upside down; if the meringue does not move, it is ready. If not, whip in 1- to 2-minute increments until stiff peaks form.

3. With a silicone spatula, fold one-third of the almond flour mixture into the meringue until just combined. In two batches, fold in the remaining almond flour mixture. The batter should flow off the spatula, slowly but continuously, in unbroken ribbons. Add the purple food coloring and lightly swirl it into the batter for a marble effect.

4. Line a 13-by-18-inch baking sheet with a silicone macaron baking mat or parchment paper.

5. Transfer the batter to a pastry bag fitted with a Wilton #12 round tip. Pipe 24 to 30 (1½-inch) circles onto the prepared baking sheet, 1 to 1½ inches apart. Gently drop the baking sheet on the counter to eliminate air bubbles and level the macarons. Dry the macarons at room temperature for 30 minutes to 2 hours, uncovered, until dull, firm, not sticky, and dry to the touch.

6. When the macarons look almost ready, position a rack in the center of the oven and preheat the oven to 300°F.

7. Bake the macarons on the center rack for 12 to 14 minutes, or until a macaron tapped on top moves only slightly.

8. Let cool for 15 to 30 minutes on a wire rack, then transfer the macarons to another tray to match similar-size shells.

9. Fill as directed in the filling recipe. Top each filled shell with another shell, then press and twist the shells together.

10. Remove from the refrigerator 30 minutes before serving.

CHANGE IT UP: Fill with Tea Whipped White Chocolate Ganache (page 195), made with Thai or dark-roast oolong tea, or Honey Lavender Whipped White Chocolate Ganache (page 196).

BLUEBERRY MATCHA LATTE MACARONS

PREP TIME: 30 minutes, plus 30 minutes to 2 hours to dry and 1 hour to refrigerate
BAKE TIME: 14 minutes
MAKES: 12 to 15 filled 1½-inch macarons

The combination of blueberries and matcha is delicious in this macaron. The bitter matcha and the sweet blueberries, as well as the chewy texture of the macarons, give these cookies a unique flavor experience that is addictive!

70 grams almond flour
48 grams powdered sugar
2 grams culinary-grade matcha powder
Pinch salt
53 grams egg whites (from about 2 medium eggs)
50 grams granulated sugar
2 drops green gel food coloring
2 drops blue gel food coloring
20 grams (1 tablespoon) blueberry jam
1 recipe Matcha Buttercream (page 179)

1. Sift the almond flour, powdered sugar, matcha powder, and salt into a small to medium bowl. Set aside.

2. In another small to medium bowl, with an electric mixer on medium-high speed, beat the egg whites for 1 to 2 minutes until frothy. While beating on medium-high speed, slowly add the granulated sugar, then beat on high speed for about 3 minutes until the mixture is thicker and white. Add the green food coloring and beat for 3 to 4 minutes until the meringue is thick, with firm, glossy peaks when you lift the beaters. Turn the bowl upside down; if the meringue does not move, it is ready. If not, whip in 1- to 2-minute increments until stiff peaks form.

3. With a silicone spatula, fold one-third of the almond flour mixture into the meringue until just combined. In two batches, fold in the remaining almond flour mixture. The batter should flow off the spatula, slowly but continuously, in unbroken ribbons. Add the blue food coloring and lightly swirl it into the batter for a marble effect.

4. Line a 13-by-18-inch baking sheet with a silicone macaron baking mat or parchment paper.

5. Transfer the batter to a pastry bag fitted with a Wilton #12 round tip. Pipe 24 to 30 (1½-inch) circles onto the prepared baking sheet, 1 to 1½ inches apart. Gently drop the baking sheet on the counter to eliminate air bubbles and level the macarons. Dry the macarons at room temperature for 30 minutes to 2 hours, uncovered, until dull, firm, not sticky, and dry to the touch.

6. When the macarons look almost ready, position a rack in the center of the oven and preheat the oven to 300°F.

7. Bake the macarons on the center rack for 12 to 14 minutes, or until a macaron tapped on top moves only slightly.

8. Let cool for 15 to 30 minutes on a wire rack, then transfer the macarons to another tray to match similar-size shells.

9. Fill as directed in the filling recipe. Add a small dab of blueberry jam in the center of the filling. Top each filled shell with another shell, then press and twist the shells together. Refrigerate for at least 1 hour, or overnight.

10. Remove from the refrigerator 30 minutes before serving.

CHANGE IT UP: Fill with Strawberry Buttercream (page 166), White Chocolate Ganache (page 197), or Mango Buttercream (page 168).

PANDAN COCONUT MACARONS

PREP TIME: 30 minutes, plus 30 minutes to 2 hours to dry and 1 hour to refrigerate
BAKE TIME: 14 minutes
MAKES: 12 to 15 filled 1½-inch macarons

Pandan, similar to a light and fragrant vanilla, is made from the pandan leaf, native to Southeast Asia. It's hard to get that flavor without an extract, so I recommend purchasing pandan extract online. Coconut powder can be found at Asian grocery stores. I like to color this macaron with a green swirl, in honor of the green pandan leaf.

70 grams almond flour

45 grams powdered sugar

5 grams coconut powder
   (I use Kara brand)

Pinch salt

53 grams egg whites (from
   about 2 medium eggs)

50 grams granulated sugar

1 gram (¼ teaspoon)
   pandan extract

2 drops green gel food
   coloring

1 recipe Pandan Coconut
   Buttercream (page 171)

1. Sift the almond flour, powdered sugar, coconut powder, and salt into a small to medium bowl. Set aside.

2. In another small to medium bowl with an electric mixer on medium-high speed, beat the egg whites for 1 to 2 minutes until frothy. While beating on medium-high speed, slowly add the granulated sugar, then beat on high speed for about 3 minutes until the mixture is thicker and white. Add the pandan extract and beat for 3 to 4 minutes until the meringue is thick, with firm, glossy peaks when you lift the beaters. Turn the bowl upside down; if the meringue does not move, it is ready. If not, whip in 1- to 2-minute increments until stiff peaks form.

3. With a silicone spatula, fold one-third of the almond flour mixture into the meringue until just combined. In two batches, fold in the remaining almond flour mixture. The batter should flow off the spatula, slowly but continuously, in unbroken ribbons. Add the food coloring and lightly swirl it into the batter for a marble effect.

4. Line a 13-by-18-inch baking sheet with a silicone macaron baking mat or parchment paper.

5. Transfer the batter to a pastry bag fitted with a Wilton #12 round tip. Pipe 24 to 30 (1½-inch) circles onto the prepared baking sheet, 1 to 1½ inches apart. Gently drop the baking sheet on the counter to eliminate air bubbles and level the macarons. Dry the macarons at room temperature for 30 minutes to 2 hours, uncovered, until dull, firm, not sticky, and dry to the touch.

6. When the macarons look almost ready, position a rack in the center of the oven and preheat the oven to 300°F.

7. Bake the macarons on the center rack for 12 to 14 minutes, or until a macaron tapped on top moves only slightly.

8. Let cool for 15 to 30 minutes on a wire rack, then transfer the macarons to another tray to match similar-size shells.

9. Fill as directed in the filling recipe. Top each filled shell with another shell, then press and twist the shells together.

10. Remove from the refrigerator 30 minutes before serving.

CHANGE IT UP: Fill with Strawberry Buttercream (page 166), Tea Whipped White Chocolate Ganache (page 195), made with Thai tea, or Passion Fruit Guava Buttercream (page 169).

PINEAPPLE COCONUT MACARONS

PREP TIME: 30 minutes, plus 30 minutes to 2 hours to dry and 1 hour to refrigerate
BAKE TIME: 14 minutes
MAKES: 12 to 15 filled 1½-inch macarons

I loved sipping piña coladas on the beach in Hawaii—what a memory. The tanginess of the pineapple and the creaminess of the coconut equaled a must-try macaron flavor for me, and now for you! I recommend a pineapple extract from Butterfly for the shell, and real pineapple juice and chunks for the buttercream.

70 grams almond flour

48 grams powdered sugar

2 grams coconut powder

Pinch salt

53 grams egg whites (from about 2 medium eggs)

50 grams granulated sugar

1 gram (¼ teaspoon) pineapple extract

2 drops yellow gel food coloring

1 recipe Pineapple Coconut Buttercream (page 170)

1. Sift the almond flour, powdered sugar, coconut powder, and salt into a small to medium bowl. Set aside.

2. In another small to medium bowl, with an electric mixer on medium-high speed, beat the egg whites for 1 to 2 minutes until frothy. While beating on medium-high speed, slowly add the granulated sugar, then beat on high speed for about 3 minutes until the mixture is thicker and white. Add the pineapple extract and beat for 3 to 4 minutes until the meringue is thick, with firm, glossy peaks when you lift the beaters. Turn the bowl upside down; if the meringue does not move, it is ready. If not, whip in 1- to 2-minute increments until stiff peaks form.

3. With a silicone spatula, fold one-third of the almond flour mixture into the meringue until just combined. In two batches, fold in the remaining almond flour mixture. The batter should flow off the spatula, slowly but continuously, in unbroken ribbons. Add the food coloring and lightly swirl it into the batter for a marble effect.

4. Line a 13-by-18-inch baking sheet with a silicone macaron baking mat or parchment paper.

5. Transfer the batter to a pastry bag fitted with a Wilton #12 round tip. Pipe 24 to 30 (1½-inch) circles onto the prepared baking sheet, 1 to 1½ inches apart. Gently drop the baking sheet on the counter to eliminate air bubbles and level the macarons. Dry the macarons at room temperature for 30 minutes to 2 hours, uncovered, until dull, firm, not sticky, and dry to the touch.

6. When the macarons look almost ready, position a rack in the center of the oven and preheat the oven to 300°F.

7. Bake the macarons on the center rack for 12 to 14 minutes, or until a macaron tapped on top moves only slightly.

8. Let cool for 15 to 30 minutes on a wire rack, then transfer the macarons to another tray to match similar-size shells.

9. Fill as directed in the filling recipe. Top each filled shell with another shell, then press and twist the shells together.

10. Remove from the refrigerator 30 minutes before serving.

CHANGE IT UP: Fill with Strawberry Buttercream (page 166), Mango Buttercream (page 168), or Vanilla Buttercream (page 164).

PASSION FRUIT GUAVA MACARONS

PREP TIME: 30 minutes, plus 30 minutes to 2 hours to dry and 1 hour to refrigerate
BAKE TIME: 14 minutes
MAKES: 12 to 15 filled 1½-inch macarons

Passion fruit and guava flavors remind me of a tropical paradise. Make these macarons if you want your taste buds to take a trip to the islands! Passion fruit and guava juices can be found in many grocery stores. The vanilla macaron shell, colored yellow with a pink swirl, complements these flavors perfectly.

70 grams almond flour

50 grams powdered sugar

Pinch salt

53 grams egg whites (from about 2 medium eggs)

50 grams granulated sugar

1 gram (¼ teaspoon) vanilla extract

2 drops yellow gel food coloring

1 drop pink gel food coloring

1 recipe Passion Fruit Guava Buttercream (page 169)

1. Sift the almond flour, powdered sugar, and salt into a small to medium bowl. Set aside.

2. In another small to medium bowl, with an electric mixer on medium-high speed, beat the egg whites for 1 to 2 minutes until frothy. While beating on medium-high speed, slowly add the granulated sugar, then beat on high speed for about 3 minutes until the mixture is thicker and white. Add the vanilla and yellow food coloring and beat for 3 to 4 minutes until the meringue is thick, with firm, glossy peaks when you lift the beaters. Turn the bowl upside down; if the meringue does not move, it is ready. If not, whip in 1- to 2-minute increments until stiff peaks form.

3. With a silicone spatula, fold one-third of the almond flour mixture into the meringue until just combined. In two batches, fold in the remaining almond flour mixture. The batter should flow off the spatula, slowly but continuously, in unbroken ribbons. Add the pink food coloring and lightly swirl it into the batter to create a marble effect.

4. Line a 13-by-18-inch baking sheet with a silicone macaron baking mat or parchment paper.

5. Transfer the batter to a pastry bag fitted with a Wilton #12 round tip. Pipe 24 to 30 (1½-inch) circles onto the prepared baking sheet, 1 to 1½ inches apart. Gently drop the baking sheet on the counter to eliminate air bubbles and level the macarons. Dry the macarons at room temperature for 30 minutes to 2 hours, uncovered, until dull, firm, not sticky, and dry to the touch.

6. When the macarons look almost ready, position a rack in the center of the oven and preheat the oven to 300°F.

7. Bake the macarons on the center rack for 12 to 14 minutes, or until a macaron tapped on top moves only slightly.

8. Let cool for 15 to 30 minutes on a wire rack, then transfer the macarons to another tray to match similar-size shells.

9. Fill as directed in the filling recipe. Top each filled shell with another shell, then press and twist the shells together.

10. Remove from the refrigerator 30 minutes before serving.

CHANGE IT UP: Fill with Strawberry Buttercream (page 166), Mango Buttercream (page 168), or Chocolate Buttercream (page 165).

RASPBERRY CHEESECAKE MACARONS

PREP TIME: 30 minutes, plus 30 minutes to 2 hours to dry and 1 hour to refrigerate
BAKE TIME: 14 minutes
MAKES: 12 to 15 filled 1½-inch macarons

Raspberry cheesecake macarons are a beautiful, yummy treat that my customers absolutely adore; in fact, I think it's one of the most popular flavors. The shells can be flavored with raspberry extract and sprinkled with graham crackers, and the coloring features a beautiful pink and white swirl.

70 grams almond flour

50 grams powdered sugar

Pinch salt

53 grams egg whites (from about 2 medium eggs)

50 grams granulated sugar

1 gram (¼ teaspoon) raspberry extract (optional)

2 drops pink gel food coloring

1½ teaspoons graham cracker crumbs

1 recipe Raspberry Cheesecake Buttercream (page 186)

1. Sift the almond flour, powdered sugar, and salt into a small to medium bowl. Set aside.

2. In another small to medium bowl, with an electric mixer on medium-high speed, beat the egg whites for 1 to 2 minutes until frothy. While beating on medium-high speed, slowly add the granulated sugar, then beat on high speed for about 3 minutes until the mixture is thicker and white. Add the raspberry extract (if using) and beat for 3 to 4 minutes until the meringue is thick, with firm, glossy peaks when you lift the beaters. Turn the bowl upside down; if the meringue does not move, it is ready. If not, whip in 1- to 2-minute increments until stiff peaks form.

3. With a silicone spatula, fold one-third of the almond flour mixture into the meringue until just combined. In two batches, fold in the remaining almond flour mixture. The batter should flow off the spatula, slowly but continuously, in unbroken ribbons. Add the food coloring and lightly swirl it into the batter for a marble effect.

4. Line a 13-by-18-inch baking sheet with a silicone macaron baking mat or parchment paper.

5. Transfer the batter to a pastry bag fitted with a Wilton #12 round tip. Pipe 24 to 30 (1½-inch) circles onto the prepared baking sheet, 1 to 1½ inches apart. Gently drop the baking sheet on the counter to eliminate air bubbles and level the macarons. Lightly sprinkle the macarons with the graham cracker crumbs. Dry the macarons at room temperature for 30 minutes to 2 hours, uncovered, until dull, firm, not sticky, and dry to the touch.

6. When the macarons look almost ready, position a rack in the center of the oven and preheat the oven to 300°F.

7. Bake the macarons on the center rack for 12 to 14 minutes, or until a macaron tapped on top moves only slightly.

8. Let cool for 15 to 30 minutes on a wire rack, then transfer the macarons to another tray to match similar-size shells.

9. Fill as directed in the filling recipe. Top each filled shell with another shell, then press and twist the shells together.

10. Remove from the refrigerator 30 minutes before serving.

CHANGE IT UP: Fill with Mango Buttercream (page 168), Vanilla Buttercream (page 164), or Strawberry Buttercream (page 166).

STRAWBERRY SHORTCAKE MACARONS

PREP TIME: 30 minutes, plus 30 minutes to 2 hours to dry and 1 hour to refrigerate

BAKE TIME: 14 minutes

MAKES: 12 to 15 filled 1½-inch macarons

I love those strawberry shortcake ice-cream bars you get from ice-cream trucks—they remind me of childhood! So, I decided to make a macaron that does just that. Using golden sandwich cookies, strawberry gelatin powder, strawberry jam, and vanilla buttercream, this macaron delivers a burst of nostalgia and flavor.

70 grams almond flour

50 grams powdered sugar

Pinch salt

53 grams egg whites (from about 2 medium eggs)

50 grams granulated sugar

1 gram (¼ teaspoon) vanilla extract

2 drops pink gel food coloring

1 tablespoon crushed golden sandwich cookies (like Golden Oreos)

1 teaspoon strawberry gelatin dessert powder (such as Jell-O)

1 recipe Vanilla Buttercream (page 164)

1½ teaspoons strawberry jam

1. Sift the almond flour, powdered sugar, and salt into a small to medium bowl. Set aside.

2. In another small to medium bowl, with an electric mixer on medium-high speed, beat the egg whites for 1 to 2 minutes until frothy. While beating on medium-high speed, slowly add the granulated sugar, then beat on high speed for about 3 minutes until the mixture is thicker and white. Add the vanilla and beat for 3 to 4 minutes until the meringue is thick, with firm, glossy peaks when you lift the beaters. Turn the bowl upside down; if the meringue does not move, it is ready. If not, whip in 1- to 2-minute increments until stiff peaks form.

3. With a silicone spatula, fold one-third of the almond flour mixture into the meringue until just combined. In two batches, fold in the remaining almond flour mixture. The batter should flow off the spatula, slowly but continuously, in unbroken ribbons. Add the food coloring and lightly swirl it into the batter for a marble effect.

4. Line a 13-by-18-inch baking sheet with a silicone macaron baking mat or parchment paper.

5. Transfer the batter to a pastry bag fitted with a Wilton #12 round tip. Pipe 24 to 30 (1½-inch) circles onto the prepared baking sheet, 1 to 1½ inches apart. Gently drop the baking sheet on the counter to eliminate air bubbles and level the macarons. Dry the macarons at room temperature for 30 minutes to 2 hours, uncovered, until dull, firm, not sticky, and dry to the touch.

6. Bake the macarons on the center rack for 12 to 14 minutes, or until a macaron tapped on top moves only slightly.

7. Let cool for 15 to 30 minutes on a wire rack, then transfer the macarons to another tray to match similar-size shells.

8. In a small bowl, stir together the cookie crumbs and strawberry gelatin powder to create a strawberry shortcake crumble.

9. Fill the shells as directed in the filling recipe. Place a dab of strawberry jam in the center of the filling and sprinkle some strawberry shortcake crumble on top. Top each filled shell with another shell, then press and twist the shells together. Refrigerate for at least 1 hour, or overnight.

10. Remove from the refrigerator 30 minutes before serving.

CHANGE IT UP: Fill with Strawberry Buttercream (page 166), Pineapple Coconut Buttercream (page 170), or Raspberry Cheesecake Buttercream (page 186).

CARROT CAKE MACARONS

PREP TIME: 30 minutes, plus 30 minutes to 2 hours to dry and 1 hour to refrigerate
BAKE TIME: 14 minutes
MAKES: 12 to 15 filled 1½-inch macarons

If you're a fan of carrot cake, this unexpected flavor will have you "hopping" for joy. The magic comes from freeze-dried carrots and cinnamon in the shell, and a decadent carrot cake–inspired cream cheese buttercream. Freeze-dried carrots can be found online easily.

5 grams freeze-dried carrots
70 grams almond flour
45 grams powdered sugar
0.31 gram (⅛ teaspoon) ground cinnamon
0.275 gram (⅛ teaspoon) ground nutmeg
Pinch salt
53 grams egg whites (from about 2 medium eggs)
50 grams granulated sugar
1 drop orange gel food coloring
1 drop brown gel food coloring
1 recipe Carrot Cake Buttercream (page 184)

1. In a food processor, pulse the freeze-dried carrots into a powder.

2. Sift the almond flour, powdered sugar, carrot powder, cinnamon, nutmeg, and salt into a small to medium bowl. Set aside.

3. In another small to medium bowl, with an electric mixer on medium-high speed, beat the egg whites for 1 to 2 minutes until frothy. While beating on medium-high speed, slowly add the granulated sugar, then beat on high speed for about 3 minutes until the mixture is thicker and white. Add the food colorings and beat for 3 to 4 minutes until the meringue is thick, with firm, glossy peaks when you lift the beaters. Turn the bowl upside down; if the meringue does not move, it is ready. If not, whip in 1- to 2-minute increments until stiff peaks form.

4. With a silicone spatula, fold one-third of the almond flour mixture into the meringue until just combined. In two batches, fold in the remaining almond flour mixture. The batter should flow off the spatula, slowly but continuously, in unbroken ribbons.

5. Line a 13-by-18-inch baking sheet with a silicone macaron baking mat or parchment paper.

6. Transfer the batter to a pastry bag fitted with a Wilton #12 round tip. Pipe 24 to 30 (1½-inch) circles onto the prepared baking sheet, 1 to 1½ inches apart. Gently drop the baking sheet on the counter to eliminate air bubbles and level the macarons. Dry the macarons at room temperature for 30 minutes to 2 hours, uncovered, until dull, firm, not sticky, and dry to the touch.

7. When the macarons look almost ready, position a rack in the center of the oven and preheat the oven to 300°F.

8. Bake the macarons on the center rack for 12 to 14 minutes, or until a macaron tapped on top moves only slightly.

9. Let cool for 15 to 30 minutes on a wire rack, then transfer the macarons to another tray to match similar-size shells.

10. Fill as directed in the filling recipe. Top each filled shell with another shell, then press and twist the shells together.

11. Remove from the refrigerator 30 minutes before serving.

CHANGE IT UP: Fill with Cream Cheese Buttercream (page 176), Chocolate Buttercream (page 165), or Cinnamon Buttercream (page 173).

CRÈME BRÛLÉE MACARONS

PREP TIME: 30 minutes, plus 30 minutes to 2 hours to dry and 1 hour to refrigerate
BAKE TIME: 14 minutes
MAKES: 12 to 15 filled 1½-inch macarons

In this recipe, you'll try your hand at creating a torched sugar top, like in crème brûlée. If you don't have a kitchen torch, you can use a kitchen lighter, but be careful, as it is not as precise. The filling is a custard buttercream—rich and creamy and perfect with the vanilla shells.

70 grams almond flour
50 grams powdered sugar
Pinch salt
53 grams egg whites (from about 2 medium eggs)
50 grams granulated sugar, plus 20 grams
1 gram (¼ teaspoon) vanilla extract
1 cup water
1 recipe Crème Brûlée Custard Buttercream (page 187)

1. Sift the almond flour, powdered sugar, and salt into a small to medium bowl. Set aside.

2. In another small to medium bowl, with an electric mixer on medium-high speed, beat the egg whites for 1 to 2 minutes until frothy. While beating on medium-high speed, slowly add the 50 grams of granulated sugar, then beat on high speed for about 3 minutes until the mixture is thicker and white. Add the vanilla and beat for 3 to 4 minutes until the meringue is thick, with firm, glossy peaks when you lift the beaters. Turn the bowl upside down; if the meringue does not move, it is ready. If not, whip in 1- to 2-minute increments until stiff peaks form.

3. With a silicone spatula, fold one-third of the almond flour mixture into the meringue until just combined. In two batches, fold in the remaining almond flour mixture. The batter should flow off the spatula, slowly but continuously, in unbroken ribbons.

4. Line a 13-by-18-inch baking sheet with a silicone macaron baking mat or parchment paper.

5. Transfer the batter to a pastry bag fitted with a Wilton #12 round tip. Pipe 24 to 30 (1½-inch) circles onto the prepared baking sheet, 1 inch apart. Gently drop the baking sheet on the counter to eliminate air bubbles and level the macarons. Dry the macarons at room temperature for 30 minutes to 2 hours, uncovered, until dull, firm, not sticky, and dry to the touch.

6. When the macarons look almost ready, position a rack in the center of the oven and preheat the oven to 300°F.

7. Bake the macarons on the center rack for 12 to 14 minutes, or until a macaron tapped on top moves only slightly.

8. Let cool for 15 to 30 minutes on a wire rack, then transfer the macarons to another tray to match similar-size shells.

9. Place the remaining 20 grams of granulated sugar in a small bowl.

10. Dip a food-safe paintbrush into the water and brush the top side of one shell in each pair with water. Dip the moistened shells in the granulated sugar to evenly coat and place them, sugared-side up, on an aluminum baking sheet or other heat-resistant surface. Use a kitchen torch to lightly torch the shells to make a crème brûlée effect. Let the brûléed shells cool for 10 minutes.

11. Fill the non-sugared shells as directed in the filling recipe. Top each filled shell with a brûléed shell, then press and twist the shells together. Refrigerate for at least 1 hour, or overnight.

12. Remove from the refrigerator 30 minutes before serving.

CHANGE IT UP: Fill with Matcha Buttercream (page 179), Espresso Buttercream (page 183), or Vanilla Buttercream (page 164).

CHOCOLATE BANANA MACARONS

PREP TIME: 30 minutes, plus 30 minutes to 2 hours to dry and 1 hour to refrigerate
BAKE TIME: 14 minutes
MAKES: 12 to 15 filled 1½-inch macarons

Chocolate and banana reminds me of warm summer days at the county fair, where I would purchase chocolate-covered frozen bananas. This macaron revisits that perfect pairing, with freeze-dried bananas and a velvety chocolate-banana buttercream.

5 grams freeze-dried banana, plus 1 teaspoon
70 grams almond flour
45 grams powdered sugar
Pinch salt
53 grams egg whites (from about 2 medium eggs)
50 grams granulated sugar
2 drops yellow gel food coloring
1 recipe Chocolate Buttercream (page 165)
1 tablespoon semisweet chocolate chips
Colored sprinkles, for decorating (optional)

1. In a food processor, pulse the 5 grams of freeze-dried banana into a powder.

2. Sift the almond flour, powdered sugar, banana powder, and salt into a small to medium bowl. Set aside.

3. In another small to medium bowl, with an electric mixer on medium-high speed, beat the egg whites for 1 to 2 minutes until frothy. While beating on medium-high speed, slowly add the granulated sugar, then beat on high speed for about 3 minutes until the mixture is thicker and white. Add the food coloring and beat for 3 to 4 minutes until the meringue is thick, with firm, glossy peaks when you lift the beaters. Turn the bowl upside down; if the meringue does not move, it is ready. If not, whip in 1- to 2-minute increments until stiff peaks form.

4. With a silicone spatula, fold one-third of the almond flour mixture into the meringue until just combined. In two batches, fold in the remaining almond flour mixture. The batter should flow off the spatula, slowly but continuously, in unbroken ribbons.

5. Line a 13-by-18-inch baking sheet with a silicone macaron baking mat or parchment paper.

6. Transfer the batter to a pastry bag fitted with a Wilton #12 round tip. Pipe 24 to 30 (1½-inch) circles onto the prepared baking sheet, 1 to 1½ inches apart. Gently drop the baking sheet on the counter to eliminate air bubbles and level the macarons. Dry the macarons at room temperature for 30 minutes to 2 hours, uncovered, until dull, firm, not sticky, and dry to the touch.

7. When the macarons look almost ready, position a rack in the center of the oven and preheat the oven to 300°F.

8. Bake the macarons on the center rack for 12 to 14 minutes, or until a macaron tapped on top moves only slightly.

9. Let cool for 15 to 30 minutes on a wire rack, then transfer to another tray to match similar-size shells.

10. Fill as directed in the filling recipe. Sprinkle the filling with some of the remaining 1 teaspoon of freeze-dried banana. Top each filled shell with another shell, then press and twist the shells together. Refrigerate for at least 1 hour.

11. Melt the chocolate chips in a microwave-safe bowl in the microwave for about 30 seconds on high power. Stir until smooth. Dip half of each macaron into the chocolate. Dust the chocolate with sprinkles (if using). Place on a silicone mat to harden, then refrigerate for 1 hour.

12. Remove from the refrigerator 30 minutes before serving.

CHANGE IT UP: Fill with Cinnamon Buttercream (page 173), Matcha Buttercream (page 179), or Strawberry Buttercream (page 166).

HAZELNUT CHOCOLATE MACARONS

PREP TIME: 30 minutes, plus 30 minutes to 2 hours to dry and 1 hour to refrigerate
BAKE TIME: 14 minutes
MAKES: 12 to 15 filled 1½-inch macarons

Hazelnut and chocolate are a perfect pair; they complement each other with their rich, distinctive flavors. I like to sprinkle these macaron shells with chopped hazelnuts and add hazelnuts to the buttercream to give it great texture.

2 grams whole hazelnuts, plus 1½ teaspoons, chopped
68 grams almond flour
50 grams powdered sugar
Pinch salt
53 grams egg whites (from about 2 medium eggs)
50 grams granulated sugar
2 drops brown gel food coloring
1 recipe Hazelnut Chocolate Buttercream (page 190)

1. In a food processor, pulse the 2 grams of hazelnuts into a powder.

2. Sift the almond flour, powdered sugar, hazelnut powder, and salt together into a small to medium bowl. Set aside.

3. In another small to medium bowl, with an electric mixer on medium-high speed, beat the egg whites for 1 to 2 minutes until frothy. While beating on medium-high speed, slowly add the granulated sugar, then beat on high speed for about 3 minutes until the mixture is thicker and white. Add the food coloring and beat for 3 to 4 minutes until the meringue is thick, with firm, glossy peaks when you lift the beaters. Turn the bowl upside down; if the meringue does not move, it is ready. If not, whip in 1- to 2-minute increments until stiff peaks form.

4. With a silicone spatula, fold one-third of the almond flour mixture into the meringue until just combined. In two batches, fold in the remaining almond flour mixture. The batter should flow off the spatula, slowly but continuously, in unbroken ribbons.

5. Line a 13-by-18-inch baking sheet with a silicone macaron baking mat or parchment paper.

6. Transfer the batter to a pastry bag fitted with a Wilton #12 round tip. Pipe 24 to 30 (1½-inch) circles onto the prepared baking sheet, 1 to 1½ inches apart. Gently drop the baking sheet on the counter to eliminate air bubbles and level the macarons. Lightly sprinkle the macarons with the remaining 1½ teaspoons of chopped hazelnuts. Dry the macarons at room temperature for 30 minutes to 2 hours, uncovered, until dull, firm, not sticky, and dry to the touch.

7. When the macarons look almost ready, position a rack in the center of the oven and preheat the oven to 300°F.

8. Bake the macarons on the center rack for 12 to 14 minutes, or until a macaron tapped on top moves only slightly.

9. Let cool for 15 to 30 minutes on a wire rack, then transfer the macarons to another tray to match similar-size shells.

10. Fill as directed in the filling recipe. Top each filled shell with another shell, then press and twist the shells together.

11. Remove from the refrigerator 30 minutes before serving.

CHANGE IT UP: Fill with Espresso Buttercream (page 183), Mocha Ganache (page 193), or Chocolate Buttercream (page 165).

WHITE CHOCOLATE MACADAMIA MACARONS

PREP TIME: 30 minutes, plus 30 minutes to 2 hours to dry and 1 hour to refrigerate
BAKE TIME: 14 minutes
MAKES: 12 to 15 filled 1½-inch macarons

Macadamia nuts remind me of the tropical beaches of Hawaii. If you don't live in a tropical paradise (I wish I did!), you can at least pretend you're there when you eat these macarons. The white chocolate complements the nutty flavor. In macaron form, it's an elevated experience!

2 grams whole macadamia nuts, plus 1 tablespoon, chopped, divided
68 grams almond flour
50 grams powdered sugar
Pinch salt
53 grams egg whites (from about 2 medium eggs)
50 grams granulated sugar
1 recipe White Chocolate Ganache (page 197)

1. In a food processor, pulse the 2 grams of macadamia nuts into a powder.

2. Sift the almond flour, powdered sugar, macadamia nut powder, and salt into a small to medium bowl. Set aside.

3. In another small to medium bowl, with an electric mixer on medium-high speed, beat the egg whites for 1 to 2 minutes until frothy. While beating on medium-high speed, slowly add the granulated sugar, then beat on high speed for 6 to 7 minutes until the meringue is white and thick, with firm, glossy peaks when you lift the beaters. Turn the bowl upside down; if the meringue does not move, it is ready. If not, whip in 1- to 2-minute increments until stiff peaks form.

4. With a silicone spatula, fold one-third of the almond flour mixture into the meringue until just combined. In two batches, fold in the remaining almond flour mixture. The batter should flow off the spatula, slowly but continuously, in unbroken ribbons.

5. Line a 13-by-18-inch baking sheet with a silicone macaron baking mat or parchment paper.

6. Transfer the batter to a pastry bag fitted with a Wilton #12 round tip. Pipe 24 to 30 (1½-inch) circles onto the prepared baking sheet, 1 to 1½ inches apart. Gently drop the baking sheet on the counter to eliminate air bubbles and level the macarons. Lightly sprinkle the macarons with 1½ teaspoons of chopped macadamias. Dry the macarons at room temperature for 30 minutes to 2 hours, uncovered, until dull, firm, not sticky, and dry to the touch.

7. When the macarons look almost ready, position a rack in the center of the oven and preheat the oven to 300°F.

8. Bake the macarons on the center rack for 12 to 14 minutes, or until a macaron tapped on top moves only slightly.

9. Let cool for 15 to 30 minutes on a wire rack, then transfer the macarons to another tray to match similar-size shells.

10. Fill as directed in the filling recipe. Sprinkle the remaining 1½ teaspoons of chopped macadamia nuts over the filling. Top each filled shell with another shell, then press and twist the shells together. Refrigerate for at least 1 hour, or overnight.

11. Remove from the refrigerator 30 minutes before serving.

CHANGE IT UP: Fill with Espresso Buttercream (page 183), Matcha Buttercream (page 179), or Chocolate Buttercream (page 165).

WHITE RABBIT CANDY MACARONS

PREP TIME: 30 minutes, plus 30 minutes to 2 hours to dry and 1 hour to refrigerate
BAKE TIME: 14 minutes
MAKES: 12 to 15 filled 1½-inch macarons

If you've never had white rabbit candy, it's a milky, creamy hard candy that turns chewy and soft. The vanilla shell is perfect with the buttercream, created from melted candies, cream, and butter. Absolutely a favorite, with a unique flavor that will wow your guests! I like to brush the shells with edible gold to give it a fancy look.

70 grams almond flour

50 grams powdered sugar

Pinch salt

53 grams egg whites (from about 2 medium eggs)

50 grams granulated sugar

1 gram (¼ teaspoon) vanilla extract

2 drops white gel food coloring

1 recipe White Rabbit Candy Buttercream (page 191)

Edible gold paint, for decorating (optional)

1. Sift the almond flour, powdered sugar, and salt into a small to medium bowl. Set aside.

2. In another small to medium bowl, with an electric mixer on medium-high speed, beat the egg whites for 1 to 2 minutes until frothy. While beating on medium-high speed, slowly add the granulated sugar, then beat on high speed for about 3 minutes until the mixture is thicker and white. Add the vanilla and food coloring and beat for 3 to 4 minutes until the meringue is thick, with firm, glossy peaks when you lift the beaters. Turn the bowl upside down; if the meringue does not move, it is ready. If not, whip in 1- to 2-minute increments until stiff peaks form.

3. With a silicone spatula, fold one-third of the almond flour mixture into the meringue until just combined. In two batches, fold in the remaining almond flour mixture. The batter should flow off the spatula, slowly but continuously, in unbroken ribbons.

4. Line a 13-by-18-inch baking sheet with a silicone macaron baking mat or parchment paper.

5. Transfer the batter to a pastry bag fitted with a Wilton #12 round tip. Pipe 24 to 30 (1½-inch) circles onto the prepared baking sheet, 1 to 1½ inches apart. Gently drop the baking sheet on the counter to eliminate air bubbles and level the macarons. Dry the macarons at room temperature for 30 minutes to 2 hours, uncovered, until dull, firm, not sticky, and dry to the touch.

6. When the macarons look almost ready, position a rack in the center of the oven and preheat the oven to 300°F.

7. Bake the macarons on the center rack for 12 to 14 minutes, or until a macaron tapped on top moves only slightly.

8. Let cool for 15 to 30 minutes on a wire rack, then transfer the macarons to another tray to match similar-size shells.

9. Fill as directed in the filling recipe. Top each filled shell with another shell, then press and twist the shells together.

10. Use a food-safe paintbrush to brush the tops of the macarons with the edible paint (if using). Refrigerate for at least 1 hour, or overnight.

11. Remove from the refrigerator 30 minutes before serving.

CHANGE IT UP: Fill with Vanilla Buttercream (page 164), Tea Whipped White Chocolate Ganache (page 195) made with Thai tea, or Matcha Buttercream (page 179).

Reindeer Toffee Macarons page 130

CHAPTER 4

Holidays and Celebrations

Birthday Cake Macarons 108

Pumpkin Pie Macarons 110

Blue with Gold Splatter Macarons 112

Pink with Gold Brush Macarons 114

Galaxy Macarons 116

Rainbow Swirl Macarons 118

Easter Egg Macarons 120

Heart Macarons 122

Ghost Pumpkin Spice
Latte Macarons 124

Snowman Eggnog Macarons 126

Bunny Macarons 128

Reindeer Toffee Macarons 130

Turkey-Shaped Hazelnut
Chocolate Macarons 132

Polar Bear Peppermint
Mocha Macarons 134

Tuxedo Macarons 136

Wedding Dress Macarons 138

BIRTHDAY CAKE MACARONS

PREP TIME: 30 minutes, plus 30 minutes to 2 hours to dry and 1 hour to refrigerate
BAKE TIME: 14 minutes
MAKES: 12 to 15 filled 1½-inch macarons

These fun, colorful macarons will be the hit at your next birthday party! The cake batter flavoring really accentuates the cake taste, along with the fluffy texture of the macarons.

70 grams almond flour
50 grams powdered sugar
Pinch salt
53 grams egg whites (from about 2 medium eggs)
50 grams granulated sugar
1 gram (¼ teaspoon) cake batter flavoring/extract
1½ teaspoons rainbow confetti sprinkles
1 recipe Vanilla Buttercream (page 164)

1. Sift the almond flour, powdered sugar, and salt into a small to medium bowl. Set aside.

2. In another small to medium bowl, with an electric mixer on medium-high speed, beat the egg whites for 1 to 2 minutes until frothy. While beating on medium-high speed, slowly add the granulated sugar, then beat on high speed for about 3 minutes until the mixture is thicker and white. Add the cake batter flavoring and beat for 3 to 4 minutes until the meringue is thick, with firm, glossy peaks when you lift the beaters. Turn the bowl upside down; if the meringue does not move, it is ready. If not, whip in 1- to 2-minute increments until stiff peaks form.

3. With a silicone spatula, fold one-third of the almond flour mixture into the meringue until just combined. In two batches, fold in the remaining almond flour mixture. The batter should flow off the spatula, slowly but continuously, in unbroken ribbons.

4. Line a 13-by-18-inch baking sheet with a silicone macaron baking mat or parchment paper.

5. Transfer the batter to a pastry bag fitted with a Wilton #12 round tip. Pipe 24 to 30 (1½-inch) circles onto the prepared baking sheet, 1 to 1½ inches apart. Gently drop the baking sheet on the counter to eliminate air bubbles and level the macarons. Sprinkle the macarons with the rainbow sprinkles. Dry the macarons at room temperature for 30 minutes to 2 hours, uncovered, until dull, firm, not sticky, and dry to the touch.

6. When the macarons look almost ready, position a rack in the center of the oven and preheat the oven to 300°F.

7. Bake the macarons on the center rack for 12 to 14 minutes, or until a macaron tapped on top moves only slightly.

8. Let cool for 15 to 30 minutes on a wire rack, then transfer the macarons to another tray to match similar-size shells.

9. Fill as directed in the filling recipe. Top each filled shell with another shell, then press and twist the shells together.

10. Remove from the refrigerator 30 minutes before serving.

CHANGE IT UP: Fill with Strawberry Buttercream (page 166), Chocolate Buttercream (page 165), or Salted Caramel Buttercream (page 178).

PUMPKIN PIE MACARONS

PREP TIME: 30 minutes, plus 30 minutes to 2 hours to dry and 1 hour to refrigerate
BAKE TIME: 14 minutes
MAKES: 12 to 15 filled 1½-inch macarons

What reminds you of fall? For me, it's a warm slice of pumpkin pie with vanilla ice cream. This macaron incorporates those fall flavors, with pumpkin pie spice in the shell and real pumpkin in the filling! The chewy macarons and creamy pumpkin and spices truly create a new flavor experience.

70 grams almond flour

48 grams powdered sugar

2 grams pumpkin pie spice

Pinch salt

53 grams egg whites (from about 2 medium eggs)

50 grams granulated sugar

2 drops orange gel food coloring

1 drop brown gel food coloring

1 recipe Pumpkin Pie Buttercream (page 185)

1. Sift the almond flour, powdered sugar, pumpkin pie spice, and salt into a small to medium bowl. Set aside.

2. In another small to medium bowl, with an electric mixer on medium-high speed, beat the egg whites for 1 to 2 minutes until frothy. While beating on medium-high speed, slowly add the granulated sugar, then beat on high speed for about 3 minutes until the mixture is thicker and white. Add the orange food coloring and beat for 3 to 4 minutes until the meringue is thick, with firm, glossy peaks when you lift the beaters. Turn the bowl upside down; if the meringue does not move, it is ready. If not, whip in 1- to 2-minute increments until stiff peaks form.

3. With a silicone spatula, fold one-third of the almond flour mixture into the meringue until just combined. In two batches, fold in the remaining almond flour mixture. The batter should flow off the spatula, slowly but continuously, in unbroken ribbons. Add the brown food coloring and lightly swirl it into the batter for a marble effect.

4. Line a 13-by-18-inch baking sheet with a silicone macaron baking mat or parchment paper.

5. Transfer the batter to a pastry bag fitted with a Wilton #12 round tip. Pipe 24 to 30 (1½-inch) circles onto the prepared baking sheet, 1 to 1½ inches apart. Gently drop the baking sheet on the counter to eliminate air bubbles and level the macarons. Dry the macarons at room temperature for 30 minutes to 2 hours, uncovered, until dull, firm, not sticky, and dry to the touch.

6. When the macarons look almost ready, position a rack in the center of the oven and preheat the oven to 300°F.

7. Bake the macarons on the center rack for 12 to 14 minutes, or until a macaron tapped on top moves only slightly.

8. Let cool for 15 to 30 minutes on a wire rack, then transfer the macarons to another tray to match similar-size shells.

9. Fill as directed in the filling recipe. Top each filled shell with another shell, then press and twist the shells together.

10. Remove from the refrigerator 30 minutes before serving.

CHANGE IT UP: Fill with Cinnamon Buttercream (page 173), Espresso Buttercream (page 183), or Salted Caramel Buttercream (page 178).

BLUE WITH GOLD SPLATTER MACARONS

PREP TIME: 30 minutes, plus 30 minutes to 2 hours to dry and 1 hour to refrigerate
BAKE TIME: 14 minutes
MAKES: 12 to 15 filled 1½-inch macarons

These macarons are perfect for a baby shower or birthday! I like gold splatter (find it online) because it's an easy design that looks high-end and classy. These can be filled with anything you like, since it's just a vanilla shell, but I recommend trying to match a color with a reminiscent flavor.

70 grams almond flour

50 grams powdered sugar

Pinch salt

53 grams egg whites (from about 2 medium eggs)

50 grams granulated sugar

1 gram (¼ teaspoon) vanilla extract

2 drops blue gel food coloring

1 recipe Tea Whipped White Chocolate Ganache (page 195), made with jasmine tea

½ teaspoon edible gold dust

¼ teaspoon vodka or vanilla extract

1. Sift the almond flour, powdered sugar, and salt into a small to medium bowl. Set aside.

2. In another small to medium bowl, with an electric mixer on medium-high speed, beat the egg whites for 1 to 2 minutes until frothy. While beating on medium-high speed, slowly add the granulated sugar, then beat on high speed for about 3 minutes until the mixture is thicker and white. Add the vanilla and food coloring and beat for 3 to 4 minutes until the meringue is thick, with firm, glossy peaks when you lift the beaters. Turn the bowl upside down; if the meringue does not move, it is ready. If not, whip in 1- to 2-minute increments until stiff peaks form.

3. With a silicone spatula, fold one-third of the almond flour mixture into the meringue until just combined. In two batches, fold in the remaining almond flour mixture. The batter should flow off the spatula, slowly but continuously, in unbroken ribbons.

4. Line a 13-by-18-inch baking sheet with a silicone macaron baking mat or parchment paper.

5. Transfer the batter to a pastry bag fitted with a Wilton #12 round tip. Pipe 24 to 30 (1½-inch) circles onto the prepared baking sheet, 1 to 1½ inches apart. Gently drop the baking sheet on the counter to eliminate air bubbles and level the macarons. Dry at room temperature for 30 minutes to 2 hours, uncovered, until dull, firm, not sticky, and dry to the touch.

6. When the macarons look almost ready, position a rack in the center of the oven and preheat the oven to 300°F.

7. Bake the macarons on the center rack for 12 to 14 minutes, or until a macaron tapped on top moves only slightly.

8. Let cool for 15 to 30 minutes on a wire rack, then transfer the macarons to another tray to match similar-size shells.

9. Fill as directed in the filling recipe. Top each filled shell with another shell, then press and twist the shells together.

10. In a small bowl, use a small food-grade paintbrush to mix the gold dust and vodka. Hold the paintbrush over the macarons in your nondominant hand. Using your dominant hand, tap the paintbrush handle so it flicks gold over the macarons. Refrigerate for at least 1 hour, or overnight.

11. Remove from the refrigerator 30 minutes before serving.

CHANGE IT UP: Fill with Matcha Buttercream (page 179) or Fruity Cereal Buttercream (page 172).

PINK WITH GOLD BRUSH MACARONS

PREP TIME: 30 minutes, plus 30 minutes to 2 hours to dry and 1 hour to refrigerate

BAKE TIME: 14 minutes

MAKES: 12 to 15 filled 1½-inch macarons

These pink with gold brush macarons are a customer favorite. They're perfect for almost any special occasion for anyone who loves pink! The gold is glamorous and fun. These macarons can be filled with any flavor—here I use White Chocolate Raspberry Ganache.

70 grams almond flour

50 grams powdered sugar

Pinch salt

53 grams egg whites (from about 2 medium eggs)

50 grams granulated sugar

1 gram (¼ teaspoon) vanilla extract

2 drops pink gel food coloring

1 recipe White Chocolate Ganache (with White Chocolate Raspberry variation; page 197)

½ teaspoon edible gold dust

¼ teaspoon vodka or vanilla extract

1. Sift the almond flour, powdered sugar, and salt into a small to medium bowl. Set aside.

2. In another small to medium bowl, with an electric mixer on medium-high speed, beat the egg whites for 1 to 2 minutes until frothy. While beating on medium-high speed, slowly add the granulated sugar, then beat on high speed for about 3 minutes until the mixture is thicker and white. Add the vanilla and food coloring and beat for 3 to 4 minutes until the meringue is thick, with firm, glossy peaks when you lift the beaters. Turn the bowl upside down; if the meringue does not move, it is ready. If not, whip in 1- to 2-minute increments until stiff peaks form.

3. With a silicone spatula, fold one-third of the almond flour mixture into the meringue until just combined. In two batches, fold in the remaining almond flour mixture. The batter should flow off the spatula, slowly but continuously, in unbroken ribbons.

4. Line a 13-by-18-inch baking sheet with a silicone macaron baking mat or parchment paper.

5. Transfer the batter to a pastry bag fitted with a Wilton #12 round tip. Pipe 24 to 30 (1½-inch) circles onto the prepared baking sheet, 1 to 1½ inches apart. Gently drop the baking sheet on the counter to eliminate air bubbles and level the macarons. Dry the macarons at room temperature for 30 minutes to 2 hours, uncovered, until dull, firm, not sticky, and dry to the touch.

6. When the macarons look almost ready, position a rack in the center of the oven and preheat the oven to 300°F.

7. Bake the macarons on the center rack for 12 to 14 minutes, or until a macaron tapped on top moves only slightly.

8. Let cool for 15 to 30 minutes on a wire rack, then transfer the macarons to another tray to match similar-size shells.

9. Fill as directed in the filling recipe. Top each filled shell with another shell, then press and twist the shells together.

10. In a small bowl, use a small food-grade paintbrush to mix the gold dust and vodka. Lightly brush the sides of the macaron all the way down the shell with the dust. Refrigerate for at least 1 hour or overnight.

11. Remove from the refrigerator 30 minutes before serving.

CHANGE IT UP: Fill with Mango Buttercream (page 168), Strawberry Buttercream (page 166), or Vanilla Buttercream (page 164).

GALAXY MACARONS

PREP TIME: 30 minutes, plus 30 minutes to 2 hours to dry and 1 hour to refrigerate
BAKE TIME: 14 minutes
MAKES: 12 to 15 filled 1½-inch macarons

Galaxy macarons are swirled with starry colors to give them a dreamy, outer-space look. Splattering them with silver creates even more depth. I fill these macarons with Cookies and Cream Buttercream, but feel free to fill them with anything you desire.

70 grams almond flour

50 grams powdered sugar

Pinch salt

53 grams egg whites (from about 2 medium eggs)

50 grams granulated sugar

1 gram (¼ teaspoon) vanilla extract

4 drops black gel food coloring

2 drops blue gel food coloring

2 drops purple gel food coloring

1 recipe Cookies and Cream Buttercream (page 175)

Silver edible paint, for decorating

1. Sift the almond flour, powdered sugar, and salt into a small to medium bowl. Set aside.

2. In another small to medium bowl, with an electric mixer on medium-high speed, beat the egg whites for 1 to 2 minutes until frothy. While beating on medium-high speed, slowly add the granulated sugar, then beat on high speed for about 3 minutes until the mixture is thicker and white. Add the vanilla and beat for 3 to 4 minutes until the meringue is thick, with firm, glossy peaks when you lift the beaters. Turn the bowl upside down; if the meringue does not move, it is ready. If not, whip in 1- to 2-minute increments until stiff peaks form.

3. With a silicone spatula, fold one-third of the almond flour mixture into the meringue until just combined. In two batches, fold in the remaining almond flour mixture. When close to fully mixed, divide the batter into three bowls. Mix the black coloring into one bowl, the purple coloring into the next bowl, and the blue coloring into the last. The batter should flow off the spatula, slowly but continuously, in unbroken ribbons.

4. Line a 13-by-18-inch baking sheet with a silicone macaron baking mat or parchment paper.

5. Transfer the batter to a pastry bag fitted with a Wilton #12 round tip: Pour the black batter into one side of the bag, the purple batter into another side, and the blue batter in yet another side to create a swirl effect. Pipe 24 to 30 (1½-inch) circles onto the prepared baking sheet, 1 inch apart. Gently drop the baking sheet on the counter to eliminate air bubbles and level the macarons. Dry the macarons at room temperature for 30 minutes to 2 hours, uncovered, until dull, firm, not sticky, and dry to the touch.

6. When the macarons look almost ready, position a rack in the center of the oven and preheat the oven to 300°F.

7. Bake the macarons on the center rack for 12 to 14 minutes, or until a macaron tapped on top moves only slightly.

8. Let cool for 15 to 30 minutes on a wire rack, then transfer the macarons to another tray to match similar-size shells.

9. Fill as directed in the filling recipe. Top each filled shell with another shell, then press and twist the shells together.

10. Using a small food-grade paintbrush, splatter the paint over the macarons, tapping the handle so it flicks silver onto the macarons. Refrigerate for at least 1 hour, or overnight.

11. Remove from the refrigerator 30 minutes before serving.

CHANGE IT UP: Fill with Toasted Almond Buttercream (page 189) or Black Sesame Buttercream (page 181).

RAINBOW SWIRL MACARONS

PREP TIME: 30 minutes, plus 30 minutes to 2 hours to dry and 1 hour to refrigerate

BAKE TIME: 14 minutes

MAKES: 12 to 15 filled 1½-inch macarons

Rainbow swirl macarons are a fun way to celebrate a birthday or any special occasion. Made with a swirl of yellow, teal, and pink, the design is festive and mesmerizing. I enjoy filling these with Fruity Cereal Buttercream to match the rainbow shell colors.

70 grams almond flour

50 grams powdered sugar

Pinch salt

53 grams egg whites (from about 2 medium eggs)

50 grams granulated sugar

1 gram (¼ teaspoon) vanilla extract

2 drops yellow gel food coloring

2 drops teal gel food coloring

2 drops pink gel food coloring

1 recipe Fruity Cereal Buttercream (page 172)

1. Sift the almond flour, powdered sugar, and salt into a small to medium bowl. Set aside.

2. In another small to medium bowl, with an electric mixer on medium-high speed, beat the egg whites for 1 to 2 minutes until frothy. While beating on medium-high speed, slowly add the granulated sugar, then beat on high speed for about 3 minutes until the mixture is thicker and white. Add the vanilla and beat for 3 to 4 minutes until the meringue is thick, with firm, glossy peaks when you lift the beaters. Turn the bowl upside down; if the meringue does not move, it is ready. If not, whip in 1- to 2-minute increments until stiff peaks form.

3. With a silicone spatula, fold one-third of the almond flour mixture into the meringue until just combined. In two batches, fold in the remaining almond flour mixture. When close to fully mixed, divide the batter into three bowls. Mix the yellow coloring into one bowl, the teal coloring into the next bowl, and the pink coloring into the last. The batter should flow off the spatula, slowly but continuously, in unbroken ribbons.

4. Line a 13-by-18-inch baking sheet with a silicone macaron baking mat or parchment paper.

5. Transfer the batter to a pastry bag fitted with a Wilton #12 round tip: Pour the yellow batter in one side of the bag, the teal batter in another side, and the pink batter in yet another to create a swirl effect. Pipe 24 to 30 (1½-inch) circles onto the prepared baking sheet, 1 inch apart. Gently drop the baking sheet on the counter to eliminate air bubbles and level the macarons. Dry at room temperature for 30 minutes to 2 hours, uncovered, until dull, firm, not sticky, and dry to the touch.

6. When the macarons look almost ready, position a rack in the center of the oven and preheat the oven to 300°F.

7. Bake the macarons on the center rack for 12 to 14 minutes, or until a macaron tapped on top moves only slightly.

8. Let cool for 15 to 30 minutes on a wire rack, then transfer the macarons to another tray to match similar-size shells.

9. Fill as directed in the filling recipe. Top each filled shell with another shell, then press and twist the shells together.

10. Remove from the refrigerator 30 minutes before serving.

CHANGE IT UP: Fill with Strawberry Buttercream (page 166), Lemon Buttercream (page 167), or Tea Whipped White Chocolate Ganache (page 195), made with jasmine tea.

EASTER EGG MACARONS

PREP TIME: 30 minutes, plus 30 minutes to 2 hours to dry and 1 hour to refrigerate
BAKE TIME: 14 minutes
MAKES: 12 to 15 filled 1½-inch macarons

Making these Easter egg macarons is a great springtime activity! They're so cute that you may want to hide them for Easter egg hunts. You can use edible ink markers to decorate the "eggs," or decorating icing—just make sure it's the kind that dries. I recommend using a silicone mat with an oval template (see Resources, page 200).

70 grams almond flour

50 grams powdered sugar

Pinch salt

53 grams egg whites (from about 2 medium eggs)

50 grams granulated sugar

1 gram (¼ teaspoon) vanilla extract

2 drops pink gel food coloring

1 recipe Strawberry Buttercream (page 166)

Edible food coloring pens or decorating icing, for decorating

1. Sift the almond flour, powdered sugar, and salt into a small to medium bowl. Set aside.

2. In another small to medium bowl, with an electric mixer on medium-high speed, beat the egg whites for 1 to 2 minutes until frothy. While beating on medium-high speed, slowly add the granulated sugar, then beat on high speed for about 3 minutes until the mixture is thicker and white. Add the vanilla and food coloring and beat for 3 to 4 minutes until the meringue is thick, with firm, glossy peaks when you lift the beaters. Turn the bowl upside down; if the meringue does not move, it is ready. If not, whip in 1- to 2-minute increments until stiff peaks form.

3. With a silicone spatula, fold one-third of the almond flour mixture into the meringue until just combined. In two batches, fold in the remaining almond flour mixture. The batter should flow off the spatula, slowly but continuously, in unbroken ribbons.

4. Line a 13-by-18-inch baking sheet with a silicone macaron baking mat or parchment paper.

5. Transfer the batter to a pastry bag fitted with a Wilton #12 round tip. Pipe 24 to 30 (1½-inch) circles onto the prepared baking sheet until the shell is almost the diameter you want, moving the bag a bit upward to create an egg shape, 1 to 1½ inches apart. Gently drop the baking sheet on the counter to eliminate air bubbles and level the macarons. Dry at room temperature for 30 minutes to 2 hours, uncovered, until dull, firm, not sticky, and dry to the touch.

6. When the macarons look almost ready, position a rack in the center of the oven and preheat the oven to 300°F.

7. Bake the macarons on the center rack for 12 to 14 minutes, or until a macaron tapped on top moves only slightly.

8. Let cool for 15 to 30 minutes on a wire rack, then transfer the macarons to another tray to match similar-size shells.

9. Fill as directed in the filling recipe. Top each filled shell with another shell, then press and twist the shells together.

10. Use the edible ink pens to make stripes, dots, and squiggles for Easter egg designs. Refrigerate for at least 1 hour, or overnight.

11. Remove from the refrigerator 30 minutes before serving.

CHANGE IT UP: Fill with Lemon Buttercream (page 167), Pineapple Coconut Buttercream (page 170), or Mango Buttercream (page 168).

HEART MACARONS

PREP TIME: 30 minutes, plus 30 minutes to 2 hours to dry and 1 hour to refrigerate
BAKE TIME: 14 minutes
MAKES: 12 to 15 filled 1½-inch macarons

Heart macarons are the perfect way to tell someone you love them! You can customize these macarons, making them any color and any flavor you like. Here, I use red velvet shells with cream cheese buttercream filling. Use a silicone mat with a heart template underneath (see Resources, page 200), or freehand it.

70 grams almond flour

45 grams powdered sugar

5 grams unsweetened cocoa powder

Pinch salt

53 grams egg whites (from about 2 medium eggs)

50 grams granulated sugar

3 drops red gel food coloring

1 recipe Cream Cheese Buttercream (page 176)

1. Sift the almond flour, powdered sugar, cocoa powder, and salt into a small to medium bowl. Set aside.

2. In another small to medium bowl, with an electric mixer on medium-high speed, beat the egg whites for 1 to 2 minutes until frothy. While beating on medium-high speed, slowly add the granulated sugar, then beat on high speed for about 3 minutes until the mixture is thicker and white. Add the food coloring and beat for 3 to 4 minutes until the meringue is thick, with firm, glossy peaks when you lift the beaters. Turn the bowl upside down; if the meringue does not move, it is ready. If not, whip in 1- to 2-minute increments until stiff peaks form.

3. With a silicone spatula, fold one-third of the almond flour mixture into the meringue until just combined. In two batches, fold in the remaining almond flour mixture. The batter should flow off the spatula, slowly but continuously, in unbroken ribbons.

4. Line a 13-by-18-inch baking sheet with a silicone macaron baking mat or parchment paper.

5. Transfer the batter to a pastry bag fitted with a Wilton #12 round tip. Pipe 24 to 30 hearts, 1½ to 1¾ inches in diameter, onto the prepared baking sheet, 1 inch apart. To pipe hearts, use your dominant hand to squeeze out the batter. Use your nondominant hand to guide the piping tip about ½ inch above the baking sheet and squeeze a heart shape from left to right. To end the heart, flick the piping tip to the side to prevent peaks on top. Gently drop the baking sheet on the counter to eliminate air bubbles and level the macarons. Dry at room temperature for 30 minutes to 2 hours, uncovered, until dull, firm, not sticky, and dry to the touch.

6. When the macarons look almost ready, position a rack in the center of the oven and preheat the oven to 300°F.

7. Bake the macarons on the center rack for 12 to 14 minutes, or until a macaron tapped on top moves only slightly.

8. Let cool for 15 to 30 minutes on a wire rack, then transfer the macarons to another tray to match similar-size shells.

9. To fill each macaron shell, squeeze a half-dollar–size swirl in the outline of the heart. Top each filled shell with another shell, then press and twist the shells together. Refrigerate for at least 1 hour, or overnight.

10. Remove from the refrigerator 30 minutes before serving.

CHANGE IT UP: Fill with Lemon Buttercream (page 167), Chocolate Buttercream (page 165), or Espresso Buttercream (page 183).

GHOST PUMPKIN SPICE LATTE MACARONS

PREP TIME: 30 minutes, plus 30 minutes to 2 hours to dry and 1 hour to refrigerate
BAKE TIME: 14 minutes
MAKES: 12 to 15 filled 1½-inch macarons

These adorable ghost macarons are almost as simple as regular macarons, just shaped more like a teardrop than a circle. The pumpkin pie spice flavor is delicious, especially with the coffee in the buttercream filling. The ghost template can be found on my blog (see Resources, page 200).

70 grams almond flour
48 grams powdered sugar
2 grams pumpkin pie spice
Pinch salt
53 grams egg whites (from
   about 2 medium eggs)
50 grams granulated sugar
1 gram (¼ teaspoon)
   vanilla extract
2 drops white gel food
   coloring
1 recipe Pumpkin Spice Latte
   Buttercream (page 185)
Edible food coloring pens
   (I use black and pink),
   for decorating

1. Sift the almond flour, powdered sugar, pumpkin pie spice, and salt into a small to medium bowl. Set aside.

2. In another small to medium bowl, with an electric mixer on medium-high speed, beat the egg whites for 1 to 2 minutes until frothy. While beating on medium-high speed, slowly add the granulated sugar, then beat on high speed for about 3 minutes until the mixture is thicker and white. Add the vanilla and food coloring and beat for 3 to 4 minutes until the meringue is thick, with firm, glossy peaks when you lift the beaters. Turn the bowl upside down; if the meringue does not move, it is ready. If not, whip in 1- to 2-minute increments until stiff peaks form.

3. With a silicone spatula, fold one-third of the almond flour mixture into the meringue until just combined. In two batches, fold in the remaining almond flour mixture. The batter should flow off the spatula, slowly but continuously, in unbroken ribbons.

4. Line a 13-by-18-inch baking sheet with a silicone macaron baking mat or parchment paper.

5. Transfer the batter to a pastry bag fitted with a Wilton #12 round tip. Pipe 24 to 30 (1½-inch) circles onto the prepared baking sheet, 1 to 1½ inches apart. Use your nondominant hand to guide the piping tip about ½ inch above the baking sheet and squeeze the batter until almost the diameter you want. To end the ghost, move your piping tip down and to the left to create a little ghost tail. Gently drop the baking sheet on the counter to eliminate air bubbles and level the macarons. Dry the macarons at room temperature for 30 minutes to 2 hours, uncovered, until dull, firm, not sticky, and dry to the touch.

6. When the macarons look almost ready, position a rack in the center of the oven and preheat the oven to 300°F.

7. Bake the macarons on the center rack for 12 to 14 minutes, or until a macaron tapped on top moves only slightly.

8. Let cool for 15 to 30 minutes on a wire rack, then transfer the macarons to another tray to match similar-size shells.

9. Fill as directed in the filling recipe. Top each filled shell with another shell, then press and twist the shells together.

10. With a black edible ink pen, make two eyes and a mouth on each macaron. Use a pink pen to create little cheeks. Refrigerate for at least 1 hour, or overnight.

11. Remove from the refrigerator 30 minutes before serving.

CHANGE IT UP: Fill with Cinnamon Buttercream (page 173), Chocolate Buttercream (page 165), or Toasted Almond Buttercream (page 189).

SNOWMAN EGGNOG MACARONS

PREP TIME: 30 minutes, plus 30 minutes to 2 hours to dry and 1 hour to refrigerate
BAKE TIME: 14 minutes
MAKES: 9 to 12 filled 2-inch macarons

Snowmen macarons are adorable and festive, especially when you use edible ink pens or decorating icing to bring them to life! I make them chubby and cute, and fill them with an Eggnog Buttercream; perfect for any winter occasion. Find the snowman template on my blog (see Resources, page 200).

70 grams almond flour

50 grams powdered sugar

1 gram (¼ teaspoon) ground cinnamon

Pinch salt

53 grams egg whites (from about 2 medium eggs)

50 grams granulated sugar

2 drops white gel food coloring

1 recipe Eggnog Buttercream (page 177)

Edible ink pens or decorating icing (I used black and orange), for decorating

1. Sift the almond flour, powdered sugar, cinnamon, and salt into a small to medium bowl. Set aside.

2. In another small to medium bowl, with an electric mixer on medium-high speed, beat the egg whites for 1 to 2 minutes until frothy. While beating on medium-high speed, slowly add the granulated sugar, then beat on high speed for about 3 minutes until the mixture is thicker and white. Add the food coloring and beat for 3 to 4 minutes until the meringue is thick, with firm, glossy peaks when you lift the beaters. Turn the bowl upside down; if the meringue does not move, it is ready. If not, whip in 1- to 2-minute increments until stiff peaks form.

3. With a silicone spatula, fold one-third of the almond flour mixture into the meringue until just combined. In two batches, fold in the remaining almond flour mixture. The batter should flow off the spatula, slowly but continuously, in unbroken ribbons.

4. Line a 13-by-18-inch baking sheet with a silicone macaron baking mat or parchment paper.

5. Transfer the batter to a pastry bag fitted with a Wilton #12 round tip. Pipe 18 to 24 (1½-inch) circles onto the prepared baking sheet, 1 inch apart. Next, pipe a smaller circle at the top of half the circles, like an uneven figure 8 for the snowman's head. Gently drop the baking sheet on the counter to eliminate air bubbles and level the macarons. Dry the macarons at room temperature for 30 minutes to 2 hours, uncovered, until dull, firm, not sticky, and dry to the touch.

6. When the macarons look almost ready, position a rack in the center of the oven and preheat the oven to 300°F.

7. Bake the macarons on the center rack for 12 to 14 minutes, or until a macaron tapped on top moves only slightly.

8. Let cool for 15 to 30 minutes on a wire rack, then transfer the macarons to another tray to match similar-size shells (1 round and 1 snowman).

9. Fill the round shells as directed in the filling recipe. Top each filled round shell with a snowman shell, then press and twist the shells together.

10. Use a black edible ink pen to make eyes and 5 dots for a coal smile. Use an orange pen to draw a carrot nose and scarf. Refrigerate for at least 1 hour, or overnight.

11. Remove from the refrigerator 30 minutes before serving.

CHANGE IT UP: Fill with Peppermint Mocha Buttercream (page 182), Toffee Filling (page 192), or Mocha Ganache (page 193).

BUNNY MACARONS

PREP TIME: 30 minutes, plus 40 minutes to 2 hours to dry and 1 hour to refrigerate
BAKE TIME: 14 minutes
MAKES: 9 to 12 filled 2-inch macarons

These bunny macarons are perfect for Easter, bunny-themed birthdays, or just an extra dose of cuteness for any occasion! The faces are made with edible ink pens, found online. I fill these with White Rabbit Candy Buttercream, since the name is fitting for the shape. Find the bunny template on my blog (see Resources, page 200).

70 grams almond flour
50 grams powdered sugar
Pinch salt
53 grams egg whites (from about 2 medium eggs)
50 grams granulated sugar
1 gram (¼ teaspoon) vanilla extract
2 drops white gel food coloring
1 recipe White Rabbit Candy Buttercream (page 191)
Edible food coloring pens (I use black and pink), for decorating

1. Sift the almond flour, powdered sugar, and salt into a small to medium bowl. Set aside.

2. In another small to medium bowl, with an electric mixer on medium-high speed, beat the egg whites for 1 to 2 minutes until frothy. While beating on medium-high speed, slowly add the granulated sugar, then beat on high speed for about 3 minutes until the mixture is thicker and white. Add the vanilla and food coloring and beat for 3 to 4 minutes until the meringue is thick, with firm, glossy peaks when you lift the beaters. Turn the bowl upside down; if the meringue does not move, it is ready. If not, whip in 1- to 2-minute increments until stiff peaks form.

3. With a silicone spatula, fold one-third of the almond flour mixture into the meringue until just combined. In two batches, fold in the remaining almond flour mixture. The batter should flow off the spatula, slowly but continuously, in unbroken ribbons.

4. Line a 13-by-18-inch baking sheet with a silicone macaron baking mat or parchment paper.

5. Transfer the batter to a pastry bag fitted with a Wilton #12 round tip. Pipe 18 to 24 (1½-inch) circles onto the prepared baking sheet, 1 to 1½ inches apart, reserving some batter for the bunny ears. Gently drop the baking sheet on the counter to eliminate air bubbles and level the macarons. Let dry at room temperature for 10 minutes, uncovered.

6. Pipe 2 oval bunny ears above half of the circles. Dry the shells at room temperature for 30 minutes to 2 hours, uncovered, until dull, firm, not sticky, and dry to the touch.

7. When the macarons look almost ready, position a rack in the center of the oven and preheat the oven to 300°F.

8. Bake the macarons on the center rack for 12 to 14 minutes, or until a macaron tapped on top moves only slightly.

9. Let cool for 15 to 30 minutes on a wire rack, then transfer the macarons to another tray to match similar-size shells (1 round and 1 bunny).

10. Fill the round shells as directed in the filling recipe. Top each filled round shell with a bunny shell, then press and twist the shells together.

11. Use a black edible ink pen to make eyes, a nose, and a mouth. Use a pink edible ink pen to color in the nose and ears. Refrigerate for at least 1 hour, or overnight.

12. Remove from the refrigerator 30 minutes before serving.

CHANGE IT UP: Fill with Lemon Buttercream (page 167), Strawberry Buttercream (page 166), or Mango Buttercream (page 168).

REINDEER TOFFEE MACARONS

PREP TIME: 30 minutes, plus 40 minutes to 2 hours to dry and 1 hour to refrigerate
BAKE TIME: 14 minutes
MAKES: 9 to 12 filled 1¾-inch macarons

Reindeer are the epitome of Christmastime—especially if one has a bright-red nose! These macarons, filled with a chewy toffee filling, will bring lots of smiles and laughs to your gatherings. They are a little more advanced in technique, but worth the effort. Find the reindeer template on my blog (see Resources, page 200).

70 grams almond flour

50 grams powdered sugar

Pinch salt

53 grams egg whites (from about 2 medium eggs)

50 grams granulated sugar

1 gram (¼ teaspoon) vanilla extract

3 drops brown gel food coloring, divided

2 drops red gel food coloring

1 recipe Toffee Filling (page 192)

Black edible ink pen, for decorating

1. Sift the almond flour, powdered sugar, and salt into a small to medium bowl. Set aside.

2. In another small to medium bowl, with an electric mixer on medium-high speed, beat the egg whites for 1 to 2 minutes until frothy. While beating on medium-high speed, slowly add the granulated sugar, then beat on high speed for about 3 minutes until the mixture is thicker and white. Add the vanilla and 1 drop of brown food coloring and beat for 3 to 4 minutes until the meringue is thick, with firm, glossy peaks when you lift the beaters. Turn the bowl upside down; if the meringue does not move, it is ready. If not, whip in 1- to 2-minute increments until stiff peaks form.

3. With a silicone spatula, fold one-third of the almond flour mixture into the meringue until just combined. In two batches, fold in the remaining almond flour mixture. When almost fully mixed, divide the batter into one medium bowl (with more batter) and two small bowls. Mix 1 drop of brown coloring into the medium bowl and the remaining 1 drop of brown coloring into a small bowl. In the remaining small bowl, mix the red food coloring. The batter should flow off the spatula, slowly but continuously, in unbroken ribbons.

4. Line a 13-by-18-inch baking sheet with a silicone macaron baking mat or parchment paper.

5. Transfer the light brown batter to a pastry bag fitted with a Wilton #12 round tip. Transfer the darker brown and red batters to two disposable piping bags, or piping bags fitted with a Wilton #3 tip. With the light brown batter, pipe 18 to 24 (1½-inch) circles onto the prepared baking sheet, 1 inch apart, reserving some batter for the reindeer ears. Gently drop the baking sheet on the counter to eliminate air bubbles and level the macarons. Dry at room temperature for 10 minutes, uncovered.

6. Using the remaining light brown batter, pipe 2 oval reindeer ears above half of the circles. Use the red batter to pipe an oval for the nose and antlers on the circle (see online template, page 200). Dry at room temperature for 30 minutes to 2 hours, uncovered, until dull, firm, not sticky, and dry to the touch.

7. When the macarons look almost ready, position a rack in the center of the oven and preheat the oven to 300°F.

8. Bake the macarons on the center rack for 12 to 14 minutes, or until a macaron tapped on top moves only slightly.

9. Let cool for 15 to 30 minutes on a wire rack, then transfer the macarons to another tray to match similar-size shells (1 round and 1 reindeer).

10. Fill the round shells as directed in the filling recipe. Top each filled round shell with a reindeer shell, then press and twist the shells together.

11. Use a black edible ink pen to draw eyes. Refrigerate for at least 1 hour, or overnight.

12. Remove from the refrigerator 30 minutes before serving.

CHANGE IT UP: Fill with Peppermint Mocha Buttercream (page 182), Chocolate Buttercream (page 165), or Espresso Buttercream (page 183).

TURKEY-SHAPED HAZELNUT CHOCOLATE MACARONS

PREP TIME: 1 hour, plus 50 minutes to 2 hours to dry and 1 hour to refrigerate

BAKE TIME: 14 minutes

MAKES: 12 to 15 filled 1½-inch macarons

For your next Thanksgiving feast, bring turkey-inspired macarons! They'll be the centerpiece of the dessert table. This design is a little difficult, so refer to the turkey template on my blog (see Resources, page 200).

70 grams almond flour

50 grams powdered sugar

Pinch salt

53 grams egg whites (from about 2 medium eggs)

50 grams granulated sugar

1 gram (¼ teaspoon) vanilla extract

3 drops brown gel food coloring

2 drops red gel food coloring

2 drops orange food coloring

2 drops yellow food coloring

1 recipe Hazelnut Chocolate Buttercream (page 190)

Black edible ink pen, for decorating

CHANGE IT UP: Fill with Toffee Filling (page 192) or Pumpkin Pie Buttercream (page 185).

1. Sift the almond flour, powdered sugar, and salt into a small to medium bowl. Set aside.

2. In another small to medium bowl, with an electric mixer on medium-high speed, beat the egg whites for 1 to 2 minutes until frothy. While beating on medium-high speed, slowly add the granulated sugar, then beat on high speed for about 3 minutes until the mixture is thicker and white. Add the vanilla and beat for 3 to 4 minutes until the meringue is thick, with firm, glossy peaks when you lift the beaters. Turn the bowl upside down; if the meringue does not move, it is ready. If not, whip in 1- to 2-minute increments until stiff peaks form.

3. With a silicone spatula, fold one-third of the almond flour mixture into the meringue until just combined. In two batches, fold in the remaining almond flour mixture. When almost fully mixed, transfer more than half the batter into a medium bowl and mix in the brown food coloring. Divide the remaining batter among three smaller bowls. Mix the red coloring into one bowl, the orange coloring into another bowl, and the yellow coloring into the last. The batter should flow off the spatula, slowly but continuously, in unbroken ribbons.

4. Line a 13-by-18-inch baking sheet with a silicone macaron baking mat or parchment paper.

5. Transfer the brown batter to a pastry bag fitted with a Wilton #12 round tip. Transfer the red, orange, and yellow batters to three disposable piping bags, or piping bags fitted with a Wilton #3 tip. With the brown batter, pipe 24 to 30 (1½-inch) circles onto the prepared baking sheet, 1 inch apart. Gently drop the baking sheet on the counter to eliminate air bubbles and level the macarons. Dry at room temperature for 10 minutes, uncovered.

6. With the red batter, pipe two upside-down teardrop shapes for feathers, spaced apart, above half of the circles. Let dry at room temperature for 10 minutes, uncovered.

7. With the orange and yellow batters, pipe more feathers between the red ones, alternating colors. Then, form a small triangle in the middle of the face for the beak.

8. Use the red batter to create a teardrop for the wattle. Dry at room temperature for 30 minutes to 2 hours, until dull, firm, not sticky, and dry to the touch.

9. When the macarons look almost ready, position a rack in the center of the oven and preheat the oven to 300°F.

10. Bake the macarons on the center rack for 12 to 14 minutes, or until a macaron tapped on top moves only slightly.

11. Let cool for 15 to 30 minutes on a wire rack, then transfer the macarons to another tray to match similar-size shells (1 round and 1 turkey).

12. Fill the round shells as directed in the filling recipe. Top each filled round shell with a decorated turkey shell, then press and twist the shells together.

13. With a black edible ink pen, draw the eyes. Refrigerate at least 1 hour, or overnight. Remove from the refrigerator 30 minutes before serving.

POLAR BEAR PEPPERMINT MOCHA MACARONS

PREP TIME: 30 minutes, plus 40 minutes to 2 hours to dry and 1 hour to refrigerate
BAKE TIME: 14 minutes
MAKES: 9 to 12 filled 1¾-inch macarons

These polar bear macarons are simple to make, and perfect for winter! The peppermint mocha filling is to die for—inspired by Starbucks' drink of the same name. Refreshing peppermint flavor, mixed with chocolate and coffee, delivers a trinity of deliciousness. Find the polar bear template on my blog (see Resources, page 200).

70 grams almond flour

50 grams powdered sugar

Pinch salt

53 grams egg whites (from about 2 medium eggs)

50 grams granulated sugar

1 gram (¼ teaspoon) peppermint extract

2 drops white gel food coloring

1 recipe Peppermint Mocha Buttercream (page 182)

Black edible ink pen, for decorating

1. Sift the almond flour, powdered sugar, and salt into a small to medium bowl. Set aside.

2. In another small to medium bowl, with an electric mixer on medium-high speed, beat the egg whites for 1 to 2 minutes until frothy. While beating on medium-high speed, slowly add the granulated sugar, then beat on high speed for about 3 minutes until the mixture is thicker and white. Add the peppermint extract and food coloring and beat for 3 to 4 minutes until the meringue is thick, with firm, glossy peaks when you lift the beaters. Turn the bowl upside down; if the meringue does not move, it is ready. If not, whip in 1- to 2-minute increments until stiff peaks form.

3. With a silicone spatula, fold one-third of the almond flour mixture into the meringue until just combined. In two batches, fold in the remaining almond flour mixture. The batter should flow off the spatula, slowly but continuously, in unbroken ribbons.

4. Line a 13-by-18-inch baking sheet with a silicone macaron baking mat or parchment paper.

5. Transfer the batter to a pastry bag fitted with a Wilton #12 round tip. Pipe 18 to 24 (1½-inch) circles onto the prepared baking sheet, 1 inch apart, reserving some batter to make the bear ears. Gently drop the baking sheet on the counter to eliminate air bubbles and level the macarons. Dry at room temperature for 10 minutes, uncovered.

6. Pipe 2 round bear ears above half of the circles. Pipe a small horizontal oval for the bear nose/muzzle onto the macaron/face. Dry at room temperature for 30 minutes to 2 hours, uncovered, until dull, firm, not sticky, and dry to the touch.

7. When the macarons look almost ready, position a rack in the center of the oven and preheat the oven to 300°F.

8. Bake the macarons on the center rack for 12 to 14 minutes, or until a macaron tapped on top moves only slightly.

9. Let cool for 15 to 30 minutes on a wire rack, then transfer to another tray to match similar-size shells (1 round and 1 bear).

10. Fill the round shells as directed in the filling recipe. Top each filled round shell with a bear shell, then press and twist the shells together.

11. Use a black edible ink pen to make two eyes and a nose (I prefer not to draw a mouth on bears, but you are welcome to). Refrigerate for at least 1 hour, or overnight.

12. Remove from the refrigerator 30 minutes before serving.

CHANGE IT UP: Fill with Espresso Buttercream (page 183), Chocolate Buttercream (page 165), or Mocha Ganache (page 193).

TUXEDO MACARONS

PREP TIME: 30 minutes, plus 30 minutes to 2 hours to dry and 1 hour to refrigerate
BAKE TIME: 14 minutes
MAKES: 12 to 15 filled 1½-inch macarons

Tuxedo macarons are the perfect addition to an engagement party, wedding shower, or actual wedding. They are simple, because they're made with a plain white macaron shell, but they do take a bit of drawing skill. Follow the design as directed (see my blog, Resources, page 200, for an online template), or create your own!

70 grams almond flour

50 grams powdered sugar

Pinch salt

53 grams egg whites (from about 2 medium eggs)

50 grams granulated sugar

1 gram (¼ teaspoon) vanilla extract

2 drops white gel food coloring

1 recipe Vanilla Buttercream (page 164)

Black edible ink pen, for decorating

1. Sift the almond flour, powdered sugar, and salt into a small to medium bowl. Set aside.

2. In another small to medium bowl, with an electric mixer on medium-high speed, beat the egg whites for 1 to 2 minutes until frothy. While beating on medium-high speed, slowly add the granulated sugar, then beat on high speed for about 3 minutes until the mixture is thicker and white. Add the vanilla and food coloring and beat for 3 to 4 minutes until the meringue is thick, with firm, glossy peaks when you lift the beaters. Turn the bowl upside down; if the meringue does not move, it is ready. If not, whip in 1- to 2-minute increments until stiff peaks form.

3. With a silicone spatula, fold one-third of the almond flour mixture into the meringue until just combined. In two batches, fold in the remaining almond flour mixture. The batter should flow off the spatula, slowly but continuously, in unbroken ribbons.

4. Line a 13-by-18-inch baking sheet with a silicone macaron baking mat or parchment paper.

5. Transfer the batter to a pastry bag fitted with a Wilton #12 round tip. Pipe 24 to 30 (1½-inch) circles onto the prepared baking sheet, 1 to 1½ inches apart. Gently drop the baking sheet on the counter to eliminate air bubbles and level the macarons. Dry the macarons at room temperature for 30 minutes to 2 hours, uncovered, until dull, firm, not sticky, and dry to the touch.

6. When the macarons look almost ready, position a rack in the center of the oven and preheat the oven to 300°F.

7. Bake the macarons on the center rack for 12 to 14 minutes, or until a macaron tapped on top moves only slightly.

8. Let cool for 15 to 30 minutes on a wire rack, then transfer the macarons to another tray to match similar-size shells.

9. Fill as directed in the filling recipe. Top each filled shell with another shell, then press and twist the shells together.

10. Use a black edible ink pen to draw two tuxedo lapels, a bow tie, and buttons in the middle of the macaron shell and fill them in. Refrigerate for at least 1 hour, or overnight.

11. Remove from the refrigerator 30 minutes before serving.

CHANGE IT UP: Fill with Chocolate Buttercream (page 165), Cookies and Cream Buttercream (page 175), or Black Sesame Buttercream (page 181).

WEDDING DRESS MACARONS

PREP TIME: 30 minutes, plus 40 minutes to 2 hours to dry and 1 hour to refrigerate
BAKE TIME: 14 minutes
MAKES: 12 to 15 filled 1½-inch macarons

As a lovely complement to the Tuxedo Macarons (page 136), these wedding dress macarons are also a great addition to wedding events! These macarons are easy to pipe, and I fill them with Raspberry Cheesecake Buttercream to match the pretty pastel pink shells. Find the wedding dress template on my blog (see Resources, page 200).

70 grams almond flour

50 grams powdered sugar

Pinch salt

53 grams egg whites (from about 2 medium eggs)

50 grams granulated sugar

1 gram (¼ teaspoon) vanilla extract

2 drops white gel food coloring

2 drops pink gel food coloring

1 recipe Raspberry Cheesecake Buttercream (page 186)

1. Sift the almond flour, powdered sugar, and salt into a small to medium bowl. Set aside.

2. In another small to medium bowl, with an electric mixer on medium-high speed, beat the egg whites for 1 to 2 minutes until frothy. While beating on medium-high speed, slowly add the granulated sugar, then beat on high speed for about 3 minutes until the mixture is thicker and white. Add the vanilla and white food coloring and beat for 3 to 4 minutes until the meringue is thick, with firm, glossy peaks when you lift the beaters. Turn the bowl upside down; if the meringue does not move, it is ready. If not, whip in 1- to 2-minute increments until stiff peaks form.

3. With a silicone spatula, fold one-third of the almond flour mixture into the meringue until just combined. In two batches, fold in the remaining almond flour mixture. When close to fully mixed, transfer some of the batter into a smaller bowl. To the original bowl, add the pink food coloring and mix well. The batter should flow off the spatula, slowly but continuously, in unbroken ribbons.

4. Line a 13-by-18-inch baking sheet with a silicone macaron baking mat or parchment paper.

5. Transfer the pink batter to a pastry bag fitted with a Wilton #12 round tip and the white batter to a piping bag fitted with a Wilton #3 piping tip. With the pink batter, pipe 24 to 30 (1½-inch) circles, 1 inch apart. Gently drop the baking sheet on the counter to eliminate air bubbles and level the macarons. Dry at room temperature for 10 minutes, uncovered.

6. With the white batter, pipe 3 white circles as the necklace and underneath that, a heart as the wedding dress bodice (see online template, page 200). Dry the macarons at room temperature for 30 minutes to 2 hours, uncovered, until dull, firm, not sticky, and dry to the touch.

7. When the macarons look almost ready, position a rack in the center of the oven and preheat the oven to 300°F

8. Bake the macarons on the center rack for 12 to 14 minutes, or until a macaron tapped on top moves only slightly.

9. Let cool for 15 to 30 minutes on a wire rack, then transfer the macarons to another tray to match similar-size shells.

10. Fill as directed in the filling recipe. Top each filled shell with another shell, then press and twist the shells together.

11. Remove from the refrigerator 30 minutes before serving.

CHANGE IT UP: Fill with Strawberry Buttercream (page 166), Fruity Cereal Buttercream (page 172), or Matcha Buttercream (page 179).

Nut-Free Chocolate Macarons page 144

CHAPTER 5

Vegan and Nut-Free Macarons and Fillings

Nut-Free Vanilla Macarons 142

Nut-Free Chocolate Macarons 144

Nut-Free Espresso Macarons 146

Nut-Free Matcha
Green Tea Macarons 148

Vegan Vanilla Macarons 150

Vegan Chocolate Macarons 152

Vegan Mint Macarons 154

Vegan Toasted Almond Macarons 156

Nut-Free/Vegan
Vanilla Buttercream 158

Nut-Free/Vegan
Chocolate Ganache 159

Nut-Free/Vegan
Strawberry Buttercream 160

Nut-Free/Vegan
Espresso Buttercream 161

NUT-FREE **VANILLA MACARONS**

PREP TIME: 30 minutes, plus 30 minutes to 2 hours to dry and 1 hour to refrigerate
BAKE TIME: 14 minutes
MAKES: 12 to 15 filled 1½-inch macarons

To make any macaron shell nut-free, replace the almond flour with oat flour or sunflower seed flour at a 1:1 ratio. These flours also give the macarons a roasted flavor that rivals nuts! You can also use the Nut-Free/Vegan Vanilla Buttercream (page 158) with these cookies if someone is also sensitive to dairy.

70 grams oat flour or sunflower seed flour
50 grams powdered sugar
Pinch salt
53 grams egg whites (from about 2 medium eggs)
50 grams granulated sugar
1 gram (¼ teaspoon) vanilla extract
2 drops white gel food coloring
1 recipe Vanilla Buttercream (page 164)

1. Sift the flour, powdered sugar, and salt into a small to medium bowl. Set aside.

2. In another small to medium bowl, with an electric mixer on medium-high speed, beat the egg whites for 1 to 2 minutes until frothy. While beating on medium-high speed, slowly add the granulated sugar, then beat on high speed for about 3 minutes until the mixture is thicker and white. Add the vanilla and food coloring and beat for 3 to 4 minutes until the meringue is thick, with firm, glossy peaks when you lift the beaters. Turn the bowl upside down; if the meringue does not move, it is ready. If not, whip in 1- to 2-minute increments until stiff peaks form.

3. With a silicone spatula, fold one-third of the flour mixture into the meringue until just combined. In two batches, fold in the remaining flour mixture. The batter should flow off the spatula, slowly but continuously, in unbroken ribbons.

4. Line a 13-by-18-inch baking sheet with a silicone macaron baking mat or parchment paper.

5. Transfer the batter to a pastry bag fitted with a Wilton #12 round tip. Pipe 24 to 30 (1½-inch) circles onto the prepared baking sheet, 1 to 1½ inches apart. Gently drop the baking sheet on the counter to eliminate air bubbles and level the macarons. Dry the macarons at room temperature for 30 minutes to 2 hours, uncovered, until dull, firm, not sticky, and dry to the touch.

6. When the macarons look almost ready, position a rack in the center of the oven and preheat the oven to 300°F.

7. Bake the macarons on the center rack for 12 to 14 minutes, or until a macaron tapped on top moves only slightly.

8. Let cool for 15 to 30 minutes on a wire rack, then transfer the macarons to another tray to match similar-size shells.

9. Fill as directed in the filling recipe. Top each filled shell with another shell, then press and twist the shells together.

10. Remove from the refrigerator 30 minutes before serving.

CHANGE IT UP: Fill with Chocolate Buttercream (page 165), Salted Caramel Buttercream (page 178), or Nut-Free/Vegan Espresso Buttercream (page 161).

NUT-FREE **CHOCOLATE MACARONS**

PREP TIME: 30 minutes, plus 30 minutes to 2 hours to dry and 1 hour to refrigerate
BAKE TIME: 14 minutes
MAKES: 12 to 15 filled 1½-inch macarons

These macarons have all the decadence of chocolate, without nuts. You can use the regular Chocolate Buttercream (page 165), or if you want to skip the dairy, the Nut-Free/Vegan Chocolate Ganache (page 159) also works perfectly. You can buy oat or sunflower seed flour, or grind the oats or seeds yourself in a food processor.

70 grams oat flour or
   sunflower seed flour
45 grams powdered sugar
5 grams unsweetened
   cocoa powder
Pinch salt
53 grams egg whites (from
   about 2 medium eggs)
50 grams granulated sugar
1 recipe Chocolate
   Buttercream (page 165)

1. Sift the flour, powdered sugar, cocoa powder, and salt into a small to medium bowl. Set aside.

2. In another small to medium bowl, with an electric mixer on medium-high speed, beat the egg whites for 1 to 2 minutes until frothy. While beating on medium-high speed, slowly add the granulated sugar, then beat on high speed for 6 to 7 minutes until the meringue is white and thick, with firm, glossy peaks when you lift the beaters. Turn the bowl upside down; if the meringue does not move, it is ready. If not, whip in 1- to 2-minute increments until stiff peaks form.

3. With a silicone spatula, fold one-third of the flour mixture into the meringue until just combined. In two batches, fold in the remaining flour mixture. The batter should flow off the spatula, slowly but continuously, in unbroken ribbons.

4. Line a 13-by-18-inch baking sheet with a silicone macaron baking mat or parchment paper.

5. Transfer the batter to a pastry bag fitted with a Wilton #12 round tip. Pipe 24 to 30 (1½-inch) circles onto the prepared baking sheet, 1 to 1½ inches apart. Gently drop the baking sheet on the counter to get rid of air bubbles and level the macarons. Dry the macarons at room temperature for 30 minutes to 2 hours, uncovered, until dull, firm, not sticky, and dry to the touch.

6. When the macarons look almost ready, position a rack in the center of the oven and preheat the oven to 300°F.

7. Bake the macarons on the center rack for 12 to 14 minutes, or until a macaron tapped on top moves only slightly.

8. Let cool for 15 to 30 minutes on a wire rack, then transfer the macarons to another tray to match similar-size shells.

9. Fill as directed in the filling recipe. Top each filled shell with another shell, then press and twist the shells together.

10. Remove from the refrigerator 30 minutes before serving.

CHANGE IT UP: Fill with Salted Caramel Buttercream (page 178), Nut-Free/Vegan Espresso Buttercream (page 161), or Nut-Free/Vegan Strawberry Buttercream (page 160).

NUT-FREE **ESPRESSO MACARONS**

PREP TIME: 30 minutes, plus 30 minutes to 2 hours to dry and 1 hour to refrigerate
BAKE TIME: 14 minutes
MAKES: 12 to 15 filled 1½-inch macarons

The roasted flavor of the oats or sunflower seed flower in these nut-free macaron shells seamlessly complements the bitterness of the coffee flavor. Pair the shells with any buttercreams or ganache you like—you can't go wrong.

70 grams oat flour or sunflower seed flour

50 grams powdered sugar

1 gram (¼ teaspoon) instant coffee

Pinch salt

53 grams egg whites (from about 2 medium eggs)

50 grams granulated sugar

1 gram (¼ teaspoon) vanilla extract

1 drop brown gel food coloring

1 recipe Espresso Buttercream (page 183)

1. Sift the flour, powdered sugar, instant coffee, and salt into a small to medium bowl. Set aside.

2. In another small to medium bowl, with an electric mixer on medium-high speed, beat the egg whites for 1 to 2 minutes until frothy. While beating on medium-high speed, slowly add the granulated sugar, then beat on high speed for about 3 minutes until the mixture is thicker and white. Add the vanilla and food coloring and beat for 3 to 4 minutes until the meringue is thick, with firm, glossy peaks when you lift the beaters. Turn the bowl upside down; if the meringue does not move, it is ready. If not, whip in 1- to 2-minute increments until stiff peaks form.

3. With a silicone spatula, fold one-third of the flour mixture into the meringue until just combined. In two batches, fold in the remaining flour mixture. The batter should flow off the spatula, slowly but continuously, in unbroken ribbons.

4. Line a 13-by-18-inch baking sheet with a silicone macaron baking mat or parchment paper.

5. Transfer the batter to a pastry bag fitted with a Wilton #12 round tip. Pipe 24 to 30 (1½-inch) circles onto the prepared baking sheet, 1 to 1½ inches apart. Gently drop the baking sheet on the counter to eliminate air bubbles and level the macarons. Dry the macarons at room temperature for 30 minutes to 2 hours, uncovered, until dull, firm, not sticky, and dry to the touch.

6. When the macarons look almost ready, position a rack in the center of the oven and preheat the oven to 300°F.

7. Bake the macarons on the center rack for 12 to 14 minutes, or until a macaron tapped on top moves only slightly.

8. Let cool for 15 to 30 minutes on a wire rack, then transfer the macarons to another tray to match similar-size shells.

9. Fill as directed in the filling recipe. Top each filled shell with another shell, then press and twist the shells together.

10. Remove from the refrigerator 30 minutes before serving.

CHANGE IT UP: Fill with Chocolate Buttercream (page 165), Salted Caramel Buttercream (page 178), or Nut-Free/Vegan Espresso Buttercream (page 161).

NUT-FREE **MATCHA GREEN TEA MACARONS**

PREP TIME: 30 minutes, plus 30 minutes to 2 hours to dry and 1 hour to refrigerate
BAKE TIME: 14 minutes
MAKES: 12 to 15 filled 1½-inch macarons

I am a huge fan of matcha green tea, and these nut-free macarons taste so delicious, you won't even know there are no almonds in them! These shells go with all types of the nut-free/vegan buttercreams or ganaches, but I chose strawberry to offset the slight bitterness of the matcha.

70 grams oat flour or sunflower seed flour

48 grams powdered sugar

2 grams (½ teaspoon) culinary-grade matcha powder

Pinch salt

53 grams egg whites (from about 2 medium eggs)

50 grams granulated sugar

2 drops green gel food coloring

1 recipe Nut-Free/Vegan Strawberry Buttercream (page 160)

1. Sift the flour, powdered sugar, matcha powder, and salt into a small to medium bowl. Set aside.

2. In another small to medium bowl, with an electric mixer on medium-high speed, beat the egg whites for 1 to 2 minutes until frothy. While beating on medium-high speed, slowly add the granulated sugar, then beat on high speed for about 3 minutes until the mixture is thicker and white. Add the food coloring and beat for 3 to 4 minutes until the meringue is thick, with firm, glossy peaks when you lift the beaters. Turn the bowl upside down; if the meringue does not move, it is ready. If not, whip in 1- to 2-minute increments until stiff peaks form.

3. With a silicone spatula, fold one-third of the flour mixture into the meringue until just combined. In two batches, fold in the remaining flour mixture. The batter should flow off the spatula, slowly but continuously, in unbroken ribbons.

4. Line a 13-by-18-inch baking sheet with a silicone macaron baking mat or parchment paper.

5. Transfer the batter to a pastry bag fitted with a Wilton #12 round tip. Pipe 24 to 30 (1½-inch) circles onto the prepared baking sheet, 1 to 1½ inches apart. Gently drop the baking sheet on the counter to eliminate air bubbles and level the macarons. Dry the macarons at room temperature for 30 minutes to 2 hours, uncovered, until dull, firm, not sticky, and dry to the touch.

6. When the macarons look almost ready, position a rack in the center of the oven and preheat the oven to 300°F.

7. Bake the macarons on the center rack for 12 to 14 minutes, or until a macaron tapped on top moves only slightly.

8. Let cool for 15 to 30 minutes on a wire rack, then transfer the macarons to another tray to match similar-size shells.

9. Fill as directed in the filling recipe. Top each filled shell with another shell, then press and twist the shells together.

10. Remove from the refrigerator 30 minutes before serving.

CHANGE IT UP: Fill with Mango Buttercream (page 168), Matcha Buttercream (page 179), or Nut-Free/Vegan Chocolate Ganache (page 159).

VEGAN **VANILLA MACARONS**

PREP TIME: 30 minutes, plus 30 minutes to 2 hours to dry and 1 hour to refrigerate
BAKE TIME: 20 minutes
MAKES: 20 to 24 filled 1½-inch macarons

If it's your first time making vegan macarons, I suggest starting with the basics, and vanilla is a great recipe to try first. You can gauge your oven, the technique, and everything in between. Making vegan macarons is similar to making regular macarons, but be sure to beat the batter thoroughly to stiff peaks, because vegan batter is thinner than regular macaron batter.

110 grams almond flour
110 grams powdered sugar
Pinch salt
75 grams aquafaba (liquid from 1 [15-ounce] can chickpeas)
0.845 grams (¼ teaspoon) cream of tartar
1 gram (¼ teaspoon) vanilla extract
70 grams granulated sugar
1 recipe Nut-Free/Vegan Vanilla Buttercream (page 158)

1. Sift the almond flour, powdered sugar, and salt into a small to medium bowl. Set aside.

2. In another small to medium bowl, with an electric mixer on medium-low speed, beat the aquafaba for 1 to 2 minutes until frothy. Add the cream of tartar and beat on medium-low speed for 30 seconds, then add the vanilla extract. While beating on medium-high speed, slowly add the granulated sugar and beat for 8 to 9 minutes until the meringue is white and thick, with firm, glossy peaks when you lift the beaters. Turn the bowl upside down; if the meringue does not move, it is ready. If not, whip in 1- to 2-minute increments until stiff peaks form.

3. With a silicone spatula, fold one-third of the almond flour mixture into the meringue until just combined. In two batches, fold in the remaining almond flour mixture. The batter should flow off the spatula, slowly but continuously, in unbroken ribbons.

4. Line a 13-by-18-inch baking sheet with a silicone macaron baking mat or parchment paper.

5. Transfer the batter to a pastry bag fitted with a Wilton #12 round tip. Pipe 40 to 48 (1½-inch) circles onto the prepared baking sheet, 1 to 1½ inches apart. Gently drop the baking sheet on the counter to eliminate air bubbles and level the macarons. Dry the macarons at room temperature for 30 minutes to 2 hours, uncovered, until dull, firm, not sticky, and dry to the touch.

6. When the macarons look almost ready, position a rack in the center of the oven and preheat the oven to 285°F. Check your oven temperature; vegan macarons are more sensitive to heat, and the feet can explode if the temperature is too hot.

7. Bake the macarons on the center rack for 18 (if your oven runs hot) to 20 minutes, or until a macaron tapped on top moves only slightly.

8. Let cool for 15 to 30 minutes on a wire rack, then transfer the macarons to another tray to match similar-size shells.

9. Fill as directed in the filling recipe. Top each filled shell with another shell, then press and twist the shells together.

10. Remove from the refrigerator 30 minutes before serving.

CHANGE IT UP: Fill with Nut-Free/Vegan Chocolate Ganache (page 159), Nut-Free/Vegan Strawberry Buttercream (page 160), or Nut-Free/Vegan Espresso Buttercream (page 161).

VEGAN **CHOCOLATE MACARONS**

PREP TIME: 30 minutes, plus 30 minutes to 2 hours to dry and 1 hour to refrigerate
BAKE TIME: 20 minutes
MAKES: 20 to 24 filled 1½-inch macarons

This recipe makes at least two dozen macarons due to their measurements; I recommend that you don't halve the recipe. Pairing it with the Nut-Free/Vegan Chocolate Ganache is a vegan chocolate lover's dream.

110 grams almond flour
102 grams powdered sugar
8 grams unsweetened
   cocoa powder
Pinch salt
75 grams aquafaba (liquid
   from 1 [15-ounce] can
   chickpeas)
0.845 grams (¼ teaspoon)
   cream of tartar
70 grams granulated sugar
1 recipe Nut-Free/Vegan
   Chocolate Ganache
   (page 159)

1. Sift the almond flour, powdered sugar, cocoa powder, and salt into a small to medium bowl. Set aside.

2. In another small to medium bowl, with an electric mixer on medium-low speed, beat the aquafaba for 1 to 2 minutes until frothy. Add the cream of tartar and beat on medium-low speed for 30 seconds. While beating on medium-high speed, slowly add the granulated sugar and beat for 8 to 9 minutes until the meringue is white and thick, with firm, glossy peaks when you lift the beaters. Turn the bowl upside down; if the meringue does not move, it is ready. If not, whip in 1- to 2-minute increments until stiff peaks form.

3. With a silicone spatula, fold one-third of the almond flour mixture into the meringue until just combined. In two batches, fold in the remaining almond flour mixture. The batter should flow off the spatula, slowly but continuously, in unbroken ribbons.

4. Line a 13-by-18-inch baking sheet with a silicone macaron baking mat or parchment paper.

5. Transfer the batter to a pastry bag fitted with a Wilton #12 round tip. Pipe 40 to 48 (1½-inch) circles onto the prepared baking sheet, 1 to 1½ inches apart. Gently drop the baking sheet on the counter to eliminate air bubbles and level the macarons. Dry the macarons at room temperature for 30 minutes to 2 hours, uncovered, until dull, firm, not sticky, and dry to the touch.

6. When the macarons look almost ready, position a rack in the center of the oven and preheat the oven to 285°F. Check your oven temperature; vegan macarons are more sensitive to heat, and the feet can explode if the temperature is too hot.

7. Bake the macarons on the center rack for 18 (if your oven runs hot) to 20 minutes, or until a macaron tapped on top moves only slightly.

8. Let cool for 15 to 30 minutes on a wire rack, then transfer the macarons to another tray to match similar-size shells.

9. Fill as directed in the filling recipe. Top each filled shell with another shell, then press and twist the shells together.

10. Remove from the refrigerator 30 minutes before serving.

CHANGE IT UP: Fill with Nut-Free/Vegan Vanilla Buttercream (page 158), Nut-Free/Vegan Strawberry Buttercream (page 160), or Nut-Free/Vegan Espresso Buttercream (page 161).

VEGAN **MINT MACARONS**

PREP TIME: 30 minutes, plus 30 minutes to 2 hours to dry and 1 hour to refrigerate
BAKE TIME: 20 minutes
MAKES: 20 to 24 filled 1½-inch macarons

For fun, I included this recipe for vegan mint macaron shells, which go great with a few fillings. See the tip for options—or get creative and make your own! I like to color the shells a mint green color, with a hint of bluish-green for visual effect.

110 grams almond flour
110 grams powdered sugar
Pinch salt
75 grams aquafaba (liquid from 1 [15-ounce] can chickpeas)
0.845 grams (¼ teaspoon) cream of tartar
1 gram (¼ teaspoon) peppermint extract
1 drop green gel food coloring
1 drop blue gel food coloring
70 grams granulated sugar
1 recipe Nut-Free/Vegan Chocolate Ganache (page 159)

1. Sift the almond flour, powdered sugar, and salt into a small to medium bowl. Set aside.

2. In another small to medium bowl, with an electric mixer on medium-low speed, beat the aquafaba for 1 to 2 minutes until frothy. Add the cream of tartar and beat on medium-low speed for 30 seconds. Add the peppermint extract and food colorings. While beating on medium-high speed, slowly add the granulated sugar and beat for 8 to 9 minutes until the meringue is thick, with firm, glossy peaks when you lift the beaters. Turn the bowl upside down, and if the meringue does not move, it is ready. If not, whip in 1- to 2-minute increments until stiff peaks form.

3. With a silicone spatula, fold one-third of the almond flour mixture into the meringue until just combined. In two batches, fold in the remaining almond flour mixture. The batter should flow off the spatula, slowly but continuously, in unbroken ribbons.

4. Line a 13-by-18-inch baking sheet with a silicone macaron baking mat or parchment paper.

5. Transfer the batter to a pastry bag fitted with a Wilton #12 round tip. Pipe 40 to 48 (1½-inch) circles onto the prepared baking sheet, 1 to 1½ inches apart. Gently drop the baking sheet on the counter to eliminate air bubbles and level the macarons. Dry the macarons at room temperature for 30 minutes to 2 hours, uncovered, until dull, firm, not sticky, and dry to the touch.

6. When the macarons look almost ready, position a rack in the center of the oven and preheat the oven to 285°F. Check your oven temperature; vegan macarons are more sensitive to heat, and the feet can explode if the temperature is too hot.

7. Bake the macarons on the center rack for 18 (if your oven runs hot) to 20 minutes, or until a macaron tapped on top moves only slightly.

8. Let cool for 15 to 30 minutes on a wire rack, then transfer the macarons to another tray to match similar-size shells

9. Fill as directed in the filling recipe. Top each filled shell with another shell, then press and twist the shells together.

10. Remove from the refrigerator 30 minutes before serving.

CHANGE IT UP: Fill with Nut-Free/Vegan Espresso Buttercream (page 161) or Nut-Free/Vegan Strawberry Buttercream (page 160).

VEGAN **TOASTED ALMOND MACARONS**

PREP TIME: 30 minutes, plus 30 minutes to 2 hours to dry and 1 hour to refrigerate
BAKE TIME: 20 minutes
MAKES: 20 to 24 filled 1½-inch macarons

The classic toasted almond macaron gets a vegan update with the delicious nutty flavor that is the star of the show. Paired with its matching buttercream, it's a winner—slightly sweet, with great depth of flavor.

110 grams almond flour
110 grams powdered sugar
Pinch salt
75 grams aquafaba (the liquid from 1 [15-ounce] can chickpeas)
0.845 grams (¼ teaspoon) cream of tartar
1 gram (¼ teaspoon) almond extract
70 grams granulated sugar
Sliced almonds, for garnish
1 recipe Nut-Free/Vegan Vanilla Buttercream (page 158)

1. Sift the almond flour, powdered sugar, and salt into a small to medium bowl. Set aside.

2. In another small to medium bowl, with an electric mixer on medium-low speed, beat the aquafaba for 1 to 2 minutes until frothy. Add the cream of tartar and beat on medium-low speed for 30 seconds, then add the almond extract. While beating on medium-high speed, slowly add the granulated sugar and beat for 8 to 9 minutes until the meringue is white and thick, with firm, glossy peaks when you lift the beaters. Turn the bowl upside down; if the meringue does not move, it is ready. If not, whip in 1- to 2-minute increments until stiff peaks form.

3. With a silicone spatula, fold one-third of the almond flour mixture into the meringue until just combined. In two batches, fold in the remaining almond flour mixture. The batter should flow off the spatula, slowly but continuously, in unbroken ribbons.

4. Line a 13-by-18-inch baking sheet with a silicone macaron baking mat or parchment paper.

5. Transfer the batter to a pastry bag fitted with a Wilton #12 round tip. Pipe 40 to 48 (1½-inch) circles onto the prepared baking sheet, 1 to 1½ inches apart. Gently drop the baking sheet on the counter to eliminate air bubbles and level the macarons. Sprinkle the macaron shells lightly with the sliced almonds. Dry the macarons at room temperature for 30 minutes to 2 hours, uncovered, until dull, firm, not sticky, and dry to the touch.

6. When the macarons look almost ready, position a rack in the center of the oven and preheat the oven to 285°F. Check your oven temperature; vegan macarons are more sensitive to heat, and the feet can explode if the temperature is too hot.

7. Bake the macarons on the center rack for 18 (if your oven runs hot) to 20 minutes, or until a macaron tapped on top moves only slightly.

8. Let cool for 15 to 30 minutes on a wire rack, then transfer the macarons to another tray to match similar-size shells.

9. Fill as directed in the filling recipe. Top each filled shell with another shell, then press and twist the shells together. Refrigerate for at least 1 hour, or overnight.

10. Remove from the refrigerator 30 minutes before serving.

CHANGE IT UP: Fill with Nut-Free/Vegan Chocolate Ganache (page 159), Nut-Free/Vegan Strawberry Buttercream (page 160), or Nut-Free/Vegan Espresso Buttercream (page 161).

NUT-FREE/VEGAN **VANILLA BUTTERCREAM**

PREP TIME: 15 minutes
MAKES: 1 cup; enough to fill 12 to 24 macarons

This vanilla buttercream is perfect for people with nut allergies, as well as vegans who prefer not to have dairy. It's quick to make and can be used as the base for any other flavors you like!

60 grams (½ stick) vegan butter, at room temperature
100 grams powdered sugar
2 grams (½ teaspoon) vanilla extract

1. In a small to medium bowl, with an electric mixer on medium-high speed, beat the butter for 2 to 3 minutes until smooth and creamy. Add the powdered sugar and beat for 3 to 4 minutes. Add the vanilla and beat at medium speed until combined.

2. Fill a piping bag (no tip required) and fill your macarons. Guide the piping bag about ½ inch above the shells and squeeze a half-dollar–size swirl on top. (The filling will spread.) To stop the filling, flick the piping tip to the side.

3. Refrigerate leftovers, covered, for up to 2 weeks, or freeze for up to 2 months. To reuse, leave at room temperature for a few hours to soften.

NUT-FREE/VEGAN **CHOCOLATE GANACHE**

PREP TIME: 5 minutes
COOK TIME: 4 minutes, plus 30 minutes to firm up
MAKES: 1 cup; enough to fill 12 to 24 macarons

This Nut-Free/Vegan Chocolate Ganache is easy to make, and it only needs two ingredients that can be found at any grocery store. Although the ingredients are slightly different than a traditional ganache, the taste is the same. Using good-quality coconut cream and chocolate makes a difference.

60 grams coconut cream
57 grams vegan semisweet
  chocolate chips

1. In a small saucepan over medium heat, heat the coconut cream for 3 to 4 minutes until almost boiling.

2. Place the chocolate in a small to medium heatproof bowl. Pour the coconut cream over the chocolate and let it sit for a minute. Whisk the cream and chocolate to blend, taking care not to leave any lumps. Refrigerate for at least 30 minutes to firm up to a smooth, thick consistency.

3. Fill a piping bag (no tip required) and fill your macarons. Guide the piping bag about ½ inch above the shells and squeeze a half-dollar–size swirl on top. (The filling will spread.) To stop the filling, flick the piping tip to the side.

4. Refrigerate leftovers, covered, for up to 2 weeks, or freeze for up to 2 months. To reuse, leave at room temperature for a few hours to soften.

NUT-FREE/VEGAN **STRAWBERRY BUTTERCREAM**

PREP TIME: 15 minutes

MAKES: 1 cup; enough to fill 12 to 24 macarons

Strawberry is one of the most loved macaron flavors, so I wanted to give you a nut-free/vegan filling recipe, too! Freeze-dried strawberries in the buttercream provide the intense fruity flavor.

60 grams (½ stick) vegan butter, at room temperature

100 grams powdered sugar

20 grams freeze-dried strawberries

1. In a small to medium bowl, with an electric mixer on medium-high speed, beat the butter for 2 to 3 minutes until smooth and creamy. Add the powdered sugar and beat for 3 to 4 minutes.

2. In a food processor, pulse the freeze-dried strawberries into a powder. Add the strawberry powder to the bowl and beat at medium speed until combined.

3. Fill a piping bag (no tip required) and fill your macarons. Guide the piping bag about ½ inch above the shells and squeeze a half-dollar–size swirl on top. (The filling will spread.) To stop the filling, flick the piping tip to the side.

4. Refrigerate leftovers, covered, for up to 2 weeks, or freeze for up to 2 months. To reuse, leave at room temperature for a few hours to soften.

NUT-FREE/VEGAN **ESPRESSO BUTTERCREAM**

PREP TIME: 15 minutes

MAKES: 1 cup; enough to fill 12 to 24 macarons

This twist on traditional buttercream might be even easier than the original recipe; no milk is needed because the vegan butter contains the necessary moisture. The coffee in this buttercream will be sure to wake you in the morning or during that afternoon slump.

60 grams (½ stick)
   vegan butter, at room
   temperature
100 grams powdered sugar
2 grams (½ teaspoon)
   instant coffee
2 grams hot water

1. In a small to medium bowl, with an electric mixer on medium-high speed, beat the butter for 2 to 3 minutes until smooth and creamy. Add the powdered sugar and beat for 3 to 4 minutes.

2. In a cup or small bowl, dissolve the instant coffee in the hot water. Pour the coffee mixture into the bowl and beat at medium speed until combined.

3. Fill a piping bag (no tip required) and fill your macarons. Guide the piping bag about ½ inch above the shells and squeeze a half-dollar–size swirl on top. (The filling will spread.) To stop the filling, flick the piping tip to the side.

4. Refrigerate leftovers, covered, for up to 2 weeks, or freeze for up to 2 months. To reuse, leave at room temperature for a few hours to soften.

Fruity Cereal Macarons
with Fruity Cereal Buttercream page 172

CHAPTER 6

Fillings

Vanilla Buttercream 164

Chocolate Buttercream 165

Strawberry Buttercream 166

Lemon Buttercream 167

Mango Buttercream 168

Passion Fruit Guava Buttercream 169

Pineapple Coconut Buttercream 170

Pandan Coconut Buttercream 171

Fruity Cereal Buttercream 172

Cinnamon Buttercream 173

Cookie Butter Buttercream 174

Cookies and Cream Buttercream 175

Cream Cheese Buttercream 176

Eggnog Buttercream 177

Salted Caramel Buttercream 178

Matcha Buttercream 179

Rose Buttercream 180

Black Sesame Buttercream 181

Peppermint Mocha Buttercream 182

Espresso Buttercream 183

Carrot Cake Buttercream 184

Pumpkin Pie/Pumpkin Spice
Latte Buttercream 185

Raspberry Cheesecake
Buttercream 186

Crème Brûlée Custard Buttercream 187

Pistachio Buttercream 188

Toasted Almond Buttercream 189

Hazelnut Chocolate Buttercream 190

White Rabbit Candy Buttercream 191

Toffee Filling 192

Mocha Ganache 193

Chocolate Mint Ganache 194

Tea Whipped White
Chocolate Ganache 195

Honey Lavender Whipped White
Chocolate Ganache 196

White Chocolate Ganache
(with White Chocolate
Raspberry variation) 197

VANILLA BUTTERCREAM

PREP TIME: 15 minutes

MAKES: 1 cup; enough to fill 12 to 24 macarons

Vanilla buttercream is the easiest flavor you can make, so make it your first recipe to solidify your foundation. You can use the buttercream as is, or customize it with any flavor you can think of! Vanilla is a flavor that also goes well with all the macaron shells. Use a high-quality vanilla extract, such as Madagascar or Mexican vanilla, for even better flavor.

113 grams (1 stick) unsalted butter, at room temperature

15 grams (1 tablespoon) milk of choice (I prefer almond milk)

1 gram (¼ teaspoon) vanilla extract

38 grams powdered sugar

PERFECT PARTNERS: Use in the Strawberry Macarons (page 34) or Chocolate Macarons (page 30).

1. In a small to medium bowl, with an electric mixer on high speed, beat the butter for about 3 minutes until creamy, white, and fluffy.

2. Add the milk and vanilla to the butter. Place the powdered sugar on top and let it absorb the liquid for about 1 minute. Beat on high speed for about another 3 minutes until fully combined.

3. Fill a piping bag (no tip required) and fill your macarons. Guide the piping bag about ½ inch above the shells and squeeze a half-dollar–size swirl on top. (The filling will spread.) To stop the filling, flick the piping tip to the side.

4. Refrigerate leftovers, covered, for up to 2 weeks, or freeze for up to 2 months. To reuse, leave at room temperature for a few hours to soften.

CHOCOLATE BUTTERCREAM

PREP TIME: 15 minutes

MAKES: 1 cup; enough to fill 12 to 24 macarons

Chocolate is a deliciously classic flavor that is super simple to make! Chocolate-loving customers really enjoy this decadent treat. It pairs well with many shell flavors, including banana, cinnamon, coffee, and vanilla.

113 grams (1 stick)
   unsalted butter, at room
   temperature

15 grams (1 tablespoon)
   milk of choice (I prefer
   almond milk)

1 gram (¼ teaspoon)
   vanilla extract

38 grams powdered sugar

4 grams (1 teaspoon)
   unsweetened cocoa powder

PERFECT PARTNERS: Use in the Chocolate Banana Macarons (page 98) or Crunchy Cinnamon Cereal Macarons (page 68).

1. In a small to medium bowl, with an electric mixer on high speed, beat the butter for about 3 minutes until creamy, white, and fluffy.

2. Add the milk and vanilla to the butter. Place the powdered sugar on top and let it absorb the liquid for about 1 minute. Beat on high speed for about 3 minutes until fully combined. Add the cocoa powder and beat for about 2 minutes until combined.

3. Fill a piping bag (no tip required) and fill your macarons. Guide the piping bag about ½ inch above the shells and squeeze a half-dollar–size swirl on top. (The filling will spread.) To stop the filling, flick the piping tip to the side.

4. Refrigerate leftovers, covered, for up to 2 weeks, or freeze for up to 2 months. To reuse, leave at room temperature for a few hours to soften.

STRAWBERRY BUTTERCREAM

PREP TIME: 15 minutes

MAKES: 1 cup; enough to fill 12 to 24 macarons

Strawberry is the number one best seller in my collection because of its simple, sweet, delicious flavor. I use freeze-dried strawberries, because they keep longer than fresh berries and they have more intense flavor. Strawberry buttercream can go with almost any macaron shell, so feel free to experiment with your favorites!

113 grams (1 stick) unsalted butter, at room temperature

15 grams (1 tablespoon) milk of choice (I prefer almond milk)

1 gram (¼ teaspoon) vanilla extract

38 grams powdered sugar

4 grams (1 teaspoon) freeze-dried strawberries

PERFECT PARTNERS:
Use in the Strawberry Macarons (page 34) or Honey Lavender Macarons (page 50).

1. In a small to medium bowl, with an electric mixer on high speed, beat the butter for about 3 minutes until creamy, white, and fluffy.

2. Add the milk and vanilla to the butter. Place the powdered sugar on top and let it absorb the liquid for about 1 minute.

3. In a food processor, pulse the freeze-dried strawberries into a powder. Add the strawberry powder to the bowl and beat on high speed for about 3 minutes until fully combined.

4. Fill a piping bag (no tip required) and fill your macarons. Guide the piping bag about ½ inch above the shells and squeeze a half-dollar–size swirl on top. (The filling will spread.) To stop the filling, flick the piping tip to the side.

5. Refrigerate leftovers, covered, for up to 2 weeks, or freeze for up to 2 months. To reuse, leave at room temperature for a few hours to soften.

LEMON BUTTERCREAM

PREP TIME: 15 minutes
MAKES: 1 cup; enough to fill 12 to 24 macarons

The lemon in this versatile buttercream is fresh, sweet, and tangy—perfect for a summer day. You can use fresh lemons in place of lemon extract, but it's much easier to use lemon extract, and it tastes just as good.

113 grams (1 stick) unsalted butter, at room temperature

15 grams (1 tablespoon) milk of choice (I prefer almond milk)

1 gram (¼ teaspoon) lemon extract

38 grams powdered sugar

PERFECT PARTNERS:
Use in the Strawberry Macarons (page 34) or Honey Lavender Macarons (page 50).

1. In a small to medium bowl, with an electric mixer on high speed, beat the butter for about 3 minutes until creamy, white, and fluffy.

2. Add the milk and lemon extract to the butter. Place the powdered sugar on top and let it absorb the liquid for about 1 minute. Beat on high speed for about 3 minutes until fully combined.

3. Fill a piping bag (no tip required) and fill your macarons. Guide the piping bag about ½ inch above the shells and squeeze a half-dollar–size swirl on top. (The filling will spread.) To stop the filling, flick the piping tip to the side.

4. Refrigerate leftovers, covered, for up to 2 weeks, or freeze for up to 2 months. To reuse, leave at room temperature for a few hours to soften.

MANGO BUTTERCREAM

PREP TIME: 15 minutes

MAKES: 1 cup; enough to fill 12 to 24 macarons

Ripe mangos are so deliciously sweet. Mango makes a great macaron flavor and can pair nicely with other fruity flavors, such as lemon or strawberry, or even matcha.

113 grams (1 stick) unsalted butter, at room temperature

15 grams (1 tablespoon) milk of choice (I prefer almond milk)

1 gram (¼ teaspoon) vanilla extract

38 grams powdered sugar

4 grams (1 teaspoon) freeze-dried mango

PERFECT PARTNERS: Use in the Passion Fruit Guava Macarons (page 88) or Strawberry Macarons (page 34).

1. In a small to medium bowl, with an electric mixer on high speed, beat the butter for about 3 minutes until creamy, white, and fluffy.

2. Add the milk and vanilla to the butter. Place the powdered sugar on top and let it absorb the liquid for about 1 minute. Beat on high speed for about 3 minutes until fully combined.

3. In a food processor, pulse the freeze-dried mango into a powder. Add the mango powder to the bowl and beat for about 2 minutes until combined.

4. Fill a piping bag (no tip required) and fill your macarons. Guide the piping bag about ½ inch above the shells and squeeze a half-dollar–size swirl on top. (The filling will spread.) To stop the filling, flick the piping tip to the side.

5. Refrigerate leftovers, covered, for up to 2 weeks, or freeze for up to 2 months. To reuse, leave at room temperature for a few hours to soften.

PASSION FRUIT GUAVA BUTTERCREAM

PREP TIME: 15 minutes

MAKES: 1 cup; enough to fill 12 to 24 macarons

When you taste this buttercream, you'll be transported to the tropics! Tangy passion fruit and guava juice impart yummy, exotic fruity flavor to the buttercream, which is delicious in fruit-flavored macaron shells.

113 grams (1 stick) unsalted butter, at room temperature

15 grams (1 tablespoon) milk of choice (I prefer almond milk)

1 gram (¼ teaspoon) vanilla extract

38 grams powdered sugar

2 grams (½ teaspoon) passion fruit puree

2 grams (½ teaspoon) guava nectar

PERFECT PARTNERS: Use in the Mango Macarons (page 38) or Strawberry Macarons (page 34).

1. In a small to medium bowl, with an electric mixer on high speed, beat the butter for about 3 minutes until creamy, white, and fluffy.

2. Add the milk and vanilla to the butter. Place the powdered sugar on top and let it absorb the liquid for about 1 minute. Beat on high speed for about 3 minutes until fully combined. Add the passion fruit puree and guava nectar and beat for about 2 minutes until combined.

3. Fill a piping bag (no tip required) and fill your macarons. Guide the piping bag about ½ inch above the shells and squeeze a half-dollar–size swirl on top. (The filling will spread.) To stop the filling, flick the piping tip to the side.

4. Refrigerate leftovers, covered, for up to 2 weeks, or freeze for up to 2 months. To reuse, leave at room temperature for a few hours to soften.

PINEAPPLE COCONUT BUTTERCREAM

PREP TIME: 15 minutes

MAKES: 1 cup; enough to fill 12 to 24 macarons

Are you a fan of piña coladas? I sure am! I get one every time I go on vacation, and this delicious tropical buttercream transports me to Cancún every time. It goes well with other fruity flavors such as strawberry or mango, as well.

113 grams (1 stick)
  unsalted butter, at room
  temperature
15 grams (1 tablespoon)
  milk of choice (I prefer
  almond milk)
1 gram (¼ teaspoon)
  vanilla extract
38 grams powdered sugar
8 grams (1½ teaspoons)
  canned pineapple tidbits
  with juice
2 grams (½ teaspoon)
  coconut powder

PERFECT PARTNERS: Use in the Mango Macarons (page 38) or Strawberry Macarons (page 34).

1. In a small to medium bowl, with an electric mixer on high speed, beat the butter for about 3 minutes until creamy, white, and fluffy.

2. Add the milk and vanilla to the butter. Place the powdered sugar on top and let it absorb the liquid for about 1 minute. Beat on high speed for about 3 minutes until fully combined. Add the pineapple and coconut powder and beat for about 2 minutes until combined.

3. Fill a piping bag (no tip required) and fill your macarons. Guide the piping bag about ½ inch above the shells and squeeze a half-dollar–size swirl on top. (The filling will spread.) To stop the filling, flick the piping tip to the side.

4. Refrigerate leftovers, covered, for up to 2 weeks, or freeze for up to 2 months. To reuse, leave at room temperature for a few hours to soften.

PANDAN COCONUT BUTTERCREAM

PREP TIME: 15 minutes
MAKES: 1 cup; enough to fill 12 to 24 macarons

Pandan is the vanilla bean of Thailand, the Philippines, and Vietnam. It is made from a green plant that has an earthy fragrance. It's subtle, but when paired with coconut, as here, it's delicious and creamy.

113 grams (1 stick) unsalted butter, at room temperature

15 grams (1 tablespoon) milk of choice (I prefer almond milk)

1 gram (¼ teaspoon) vanilla extract

38 grams powdered sugar

2 grams (½ teaspoon) pandan extract

2 grams (½ teaspoon) coconut powder

PERFECT PARTNERS: Use in the Mango Macarons (page 38) or Matcha Green Tea Macarons (page 48).

1. In a small to medium bowl, with an electric mixer on high speed, beat the butter for about 3 minutes until creamy, white, and fluffy.

2. Add the milk and vanilla to the butter. Place the powdered sugar on top and let it absorb the liquid for about 1 minute. Beat on high speed for about 3 minutes until fully combined. Add the pandan extract and coconut powder and beat for about 2 minutes until combined.

3. Fill a piping bag (no tip required) and fill your macarons. Guide the piping bag about ½ inch above the shells and squeeze a half-dollar–size swirl on top. (The filling will spread.) To stop the filling, flick the piping tip to the side.

4. Refrigerate leftovers, covered, for up to 2 weeks, or freeze for up to 2 months. To reuse, leave at room temperature for a few hours to soften.

FRUITY CEREAL BUTTERCREAM

PREP TIME: 15 minutes

MAKES: 1 cup; enough to fill 12 to 24 macarons

Fruity cereal reminds me of my childhood and Saturday mornings spent watching cartoons while eating this sweet, fruity, crunchy treat. That's what you'll imagine when you try this buttercream! It's one of my customers' all-time favorites, and especially a hit with kids.

113 grams (1 stick)
   unsalted butter, at room
   temperature

15 grams (1 tablespoon)
   milk of choice (I prefer
   almond milk)

1 gram (¼ teaspoon)
   vanilla extract

38 grams powdered sugar

50 grams fruity cereal
   of choice

PERFECT PARTNERS:
Use in the Strawberry
Macarons (page 34)
or Mango Macarons
(page 38).

1. In a small to medium bowl, with an electric mixer on high speed, beat the butter for about 3 minutes until creamy, white, and fluffy.

2. Add the milk and vanilla to the butter. Place the powdered sugar on top and let it absorb the liquid for about 1 minute. Beat on high speed for about 3 minutes until fully combined.

3. In a food processor, pulse the fruity cereal into a powder. Add the cereal powder to the bowl and beat for about 2 minutes until combined.

4. Fill a piping bag (no tip required) and fill your macarons. Guide the piping bag about ½ inch above the shells and squeeze a half-dollar–size swirl on top. (The filling will spread.) To stop the filling, flick the piping tip to the side.

5. Refrigerate leftovers, covered, for up to 2 weeks, or freeze for up to 2 months. To reuse, leave at room temperature for a few hours to soften.

CINNAMON BUTTERCREAM

PREP TIME: 15 minutes
MAKES: 1 cup; enough to fill 12 to 24 macarons

Cinnamon reminds me of the holidays—warm, festive, and spicy. This buttercream pairs well with fruit or chocolate flavors, and it is a snap to make! I like to add a piece of Cinnamon Toast Crunch cereal between the filled shells for added texture.

113 grams (1 stick)
   unsalted butter, at room
   temperature
15 grams (1 tablespoon)
   milk of choice (I prefer
   almond milk)
1 gram (¼ teaspoon)
   vanilla extract
38 grams powdered sugar
2 grams (½ teaspoon)
   ground cinnamon

PERFECT PARTNERS: Use in the Chocolate Banana Macarons (page 98) or Toasted Almond Macarons (page 42).

1. In a small to medium bowl, with an electric mixer on high speed, beat the butter for about 3 minutes until creamy, white, and fluffy.

2. Add the milk and vanilla to the butter. Place the powdered sugar on top and let it absorb the liquid for about 1 minute. Beat on high speed for about 3 minutes until fully combined. Add the cinnamon and beat for 2 minutes until combined.

3. Fill a piping bag (no tip required) and fill your macarons. Guide the piping bag about ½ inch above the shells and squeeze a half-dollar–size swirl on top. (The filling will spread.) To stop the filling, flick the piping tip to the side.

4. Refrigerate leftovers, covered, for up to 2 weeks, or freeze for up to 2 months. To reuse, leave at room temperature for a few hours to soften.

COOKIE BUTTER BUTTERCREAM

PREP TIME: 15 minutes
MAKES: 1 cup; enough to fill 12 to 24 macarons

Have you tried Biscoff spread, Speculoos spread, or Trader Joe's Cookie Butter? They're yummy blends of cookies and spices in spreadable butter form. This cookie butter buttercream adds a delicious flavor to a macaron.

113 grams (1 stick) unsalted butter, at room temperature
15 grams (1 tablespoon) milk of choice (I prefer almond milk)
1 gram (¼ teaspoon) vanilla extract
38 grams powdered sugar
8 grams (2 teaspoons) cookie butter spread

PERFECT PARTNERS: Use in the Crunchy Cinnamon Cereal Macarons (page 68) or Carrot Cake Macarons (page 94).

1. In a small to medium bowl, with an electric mixer on high speed, beat the butter for about 3 minutes until creamy, white, and fluffy.

2. Add the milk and vanilla to the butter. Place the powdered sugar on top and let it absorb the liquid for about 1 minute. Beat on high speed for about 3 minutes until fully combined. Add the cookie butter spread and beat for about 2 minutes until combined.

3. Fill a piping bag (no tip required) and fill your macarons. Guide the piping bag about ½ inch above the shells and squeeze a half-dollar–size swirl on top. (The filling will spread.) To stop the filling, flick the piping tip to the side.

4. Refrigerate leftovers, covered, for up to 2 weeks, or freeze for up to 2 months. To reuse, leave at room temperature for a few hours to soften.

COOKIES AND CREAM BUTTERCREAM

PREP TIME: 15 minutes

MAKES: 1 cup; enough to fill 12 to 24 macarons

Putting Oreos into our easy vanilla buttercream base makes it taste like cookies and cream ice cream. It's one of my most popular flavors, and once you try it, you'll be wondering how you lived this long without it!

113 grams (1 stick)
   unsalted butter, at room
   temperature
15 grams (1 tablespoon)
   milk of choice (I prefer
   almond milk)
1 gram (¼ teaspoon)
   vanilla extract
38 grams powdered sugar
50 grams (½ cup)
   Oreo cookies

PERFECT PARTNERS:
Use in the Matcha Green
Tea Macarons (page 48)
or Chocolate Macarons
(page 30).

1. In a small to medium bowl, with an electric mixer on high speed, beat the butter for about 3 minutes until creamy, white, and fluffy.

2. Add the milk and vanilla to the butter. Place the powdered sugar on top and let it absorb the liquid for about 1 minute. Beat on high speed for about 3 minutes until fully combined.

3. In a food processor, pulse the Oreos into a powder. Add the Oreo powder to the bowl and beat for about 2 minutes until combined.

4. Fill a piping bag (no tip required) and fill your macarons. Guide the piping bag about ½ inch above the shells and squeeze a half-dollar–size swirl on top. (The filling will spread.) To stop the filling, flick the piping tip to the side.

5. Refrigerate leftovers, covered, for up to 2 weeks, or freeze for up to 2 months. To reuse, leave at room temperature for a few hours to soften.

CREAM CHEESE BUTTERCREAM

PREP TIME: 15 minutes

MAKES: 1 cup; enough to fill 12 to 24 macarons

The tangy, creamy sweetness in this buttercream is irresistible, especially if you love cream cheese. It is simple to make and pairs well with many macaron shells.

85 grams (¾ stick) unsalted butter, at room temperature

28 grams (2 tablespoons) cream cheese, at room temperature

1 gram (¼ teaspoon) vanilla extract

38 grams powdered sugar

PERFECT PARTNERS:
Use in the Carrot Cake Macarons (page 94) or Strawberry Macarons (page 34).

1. In a small to medium bowl, with an electric mixer on high speed, beat the butter and cream cheese for about 3 minutes until creamy, white, and fluffy.

2. Add the vanilla to the butter and cream cheese. Place the powdered sugar on top and let it absorb the liquid for about 1 minute. Beat on high speed for about 3 minutes until fully combined.

3. Fill a piping bag (no tip required) and fill your macarons. Guide the piping bag about ½ inch above the shells and squeeze a half-dollar–size swirl on top. (The filling will spread.) To stop the filling, flick the piping tip to the side.

4. Refrigerate leftovers, covered, for up to 2 weeks, or freeze for up to 2 months. To reuse, leave at room temperature for a few hours to soften.

EGGNOG BUTTERCREAM

PREP TIME: 15 minutes

MAKES: 1 cup; enough to fill 12 to 24 macarons

Warmly spiced eggnog, with its cinnamon and nutmeg flavors, is a special treat during the holidays. This recipe uses eggnog in place of milk to keep it rich and creamy.

113 grams (1 stick)
   unsalted butter, at room
   temperature
15 grams (1 tablespoon)
   eggnog
1 gram (¼ teaspoon)
   vanilla extract
38 grams powdered sugar
1 gram (¼ teaspoon)
   ground nutmeg
1 gram (¼ teaspoon) ground
   cinnamon

PERFECT PARTNERS:
Use in the Carrot Cake
Macarons (page 94) or
Crunchy Cinnamon Cereal
Macarons (page 68).

1. In a small to medium bowl, with an electric mixer on high speed, beat the butter for about 3 minutes until creamy, white, and fluffy.

2. Add the eggnog and vanilla to the butter. Place the powdered sugar on top and let it absorb the liquid for about 1 minute. Beat on high speed for about 3 minutes until fully combined. Add the nutmeg and cinnamon and beat for 2 minutes until combined.

3. Fill a piping bag (no tip required) and fill your macarons. Guide the piping bag about ½ inch above the shells and squeeze a half-dollar–size swirl on top. (The filling will spread.) To stop the filling, flick the piping tip to the side.

4. Refrigerate leftovers, covered, for up to 2 weeks, or freeze for up to 2 months. To reuse, leave at room temperature for a few hours to soften.

SALTED CARAMEL BUTTERCREAM

PREP TIME: 15 minutes

MAKES: 1 cup; enough to fill 12 to 24 macarons

This salted caramel buttercream is easy and delicious and imparts a rich flavor to the macarons without much effort. The sweetness from the caramel sauce is enough without adding any extra sugar, while the sea salt balances the sweetness and gives the caramel depth.

113 grams (1 stick)
   unsalted butter, at room
   temperature
80 grams caramel sauce
3 grams sea salt

PERFECT PARTNERS:
Use in the Pistachio
Macarons (page 44) or
Honey Lavender Macarons
(page 50).

1. In a small to medium bowl, with an electric mixer on high speed, beat the butter for about 3 minutes until creamy, white, and fluffy.

2. Add the caramel sauce and salt to the butter. Beat on high speed for about 3 minutes until fully combined. The buttercream may separate at first, but keep whipping, it will come together.

3. Fill a piping bag (no tip required) and fill your macarons. Guide the piping bag about ½ inch above the shells and squeeze a half-dollar–size swirl on top. (The filling will spread.) To stop the filling, flick the piping tip to the side.

4. Refrigerate leftovers, covered, for up to 2 weeks, or freeze for up to 2 months. To reuse, leave at room temperature for a few hours to soften.

MATCHA BUTTERCREAM

PREP TIME: 15 minutes

MAKES: 1 cup; enough to fill 12 to 24 macarons

Matcha is slightly bitter and earthy, but also smooth and creamy. A matcha latte in the morning delivers just the right amount of caffeine. This buttercream works so well in many combinations, like with blueberry, chocolate, cookies and cream, raspberry, and strawberry shells, and more.

113 grams (1 stick)
   unsalted butter, at room
   temperature

15 grams (1 tablespoon)
   milk of choice (I prefer
   almond milk)

1 gram (¼ teaspoon)
   vanilla extract

38 grams powdered sugar

2 grams (½ teaspoon)
   culinary-grade
   matcha powder

PERFECT PARTNERS:
Use in the Strawberry Macarons (page 34) or Cookies and Cream Macarons (page 72).

1. In a small to medium bowl, with an electric mixer on high speed, beat the butter for about 3 minutes until creamy, white, and fluffy.

2. Add the milk and vanilla to the butter. Place the powdered sugar on top and let it absorb the liquid for about 1 minute. Beat on high speed for about 3 minutes until fully combined. Add the matcha powder and beat for about 2 minutes until combined.

3. Fill a piping bag (no tip required) and fill your macarons. Guide the piping bag about ½ inch above the shells and squeeze a half-dollar–size swirl on top. (The filling will spread.) To stop the filling, flick the piping tip to the side.

4. Refrigerate leftovers, covered, for up to 2 weeks, or freeze for up to 2 months. To reuse, leave at room temperature for a few hours to soften.

ROSE BUTTERCREAM

PREP TIME: 15 minutes

MAKES: 1 cup; enough to fill 12 to 24 macarons

The sweet, floral fragrance of rose in a macaron is beautiful and traditional in French pâtisseries. It's a sophisticated flavor, like lavender, and goes well with fruity flavors like strawberry or lemon.

113 grams (1 stick) unsalted butter, at room temperature

15 grams (1 tablespoon) milk of choice (I prefer almond milk)

1 gram (¼ teaspoon) vanilla extract

1 gram (¼ teaspoon) rose extract or rose water

38 grams powdered sugar

PERFECT PARTNERS: Use in the Lemon Macarons (page 32) or Strawberry Macarons (page 34).

1. In a small to medium bowl, with an electric mixer on high speed, beat the butter for about 3 minutes until creamy, white, and fluffy.

2. Add the milk, vanilla, and rose extract to the butter. Place the powdered sugar on top and let it absorb the liquid for about 1 minute. Beat on high speed for about 3 minutes until fully combined.

3. Fill a piping bag (no tip required) and fill your macarons. Guide the piping bag about ½ inch above the shells and squeeze a half-dollar–size swirl on top. (The filling will spread.) To stop the filling, flick the piping tip to the side.

4. Refrigerate leftovers, covered, for up to 2 weeks, or freeze for up to 2 months. To reuse, leave at room temperature for a few hours to soften.

BLACK SESAME BUTTERCREAM

PREP TIME: 15 minutes

MAKES: 1 cup; enough to fill 12 to 24 macarons

Black sesame has an earthy, nutty taste that goes well with umami flavors, like matcha, or rich flavors, like chocolate. It's definitely unique, and you should try it if you are into black sesame. It gives the buttercream a gray speckled color and blends perfectly with the vanilla buttercream base.

113 grams (1 stick) unsalted butter, at room temperature

15 grams (1 tablespoon) milk of choice (I prefer almond milk)

1 gram (¼ teaspoon) vanilla extract

38 grams powdered sugar

4 grams (1 teaspoon) black sesame powder

PERFECT PARTNERS: Use in the Matcha Green Tea Macarons (page 48) or Toasted Almond Macarons (page 42).

1. In a small to medium bowl, with an electric mixer on high speed, beat the butter for about 3 minutes until creamy, white, and fluffy.

2. Add the milk and vanilla to the butter. Place the powdered sugar on top and let it absorb the liquid for about 1 minute. Beat on high speed for about 3 minutes until fully combined. Add the black sesame powder and beat for about 2 minutes until combined.

3. Fill a piping bag (no tip required) and fill your macarons. Guide the piping bag about ½ inch above the shells and squeeze a half-dollar-size swirl on top. (The filling will spread.) To stop the filling, flick the piping tip to the side.

4. Refrigerate leftovers, covered, for up to 2 weeks, or freeze for up to 2 months. To reuse, leave at room temperature for a few hours to soften.

PEPPERMINT MOCHA BUTTERCREAM

PREP TIME: 15 minutes

MAKES: 1 cup; enough to fill 12 to 24 macarons

When I go to coffee shops around the holidays, I like to order a hot peppermint mocha, which makes me feel all warm and fuzzy. This buttercream is inspired by the delightful combination of coffee, chocolate, and peppermint, and truly captures it in macaron form.

113 grams (1 stick) unsalted butter, at room temperature

15 grams (1 tablespoon) milk of choice (I prefer almond milk)

1 gram (¼ teaspoon) peppermint extract

38 grams powdered sugar

2 grams (½ teaspoon) instant coffee

1 gram (¼ teaspoon) hot water

2 grams (½ teaspoon) unsweetened cocoa powder

PERFECT PARTNERS: Use in the Chocolate Mint Macarons (page 40) or Snowman Eggnog Macarons (page 126).

1. In a small to medium bowl, with an electric mixer on high speed, beat the butter for about 3 minutes until creamy, white, and fluffy.

2. Add the milk and peppermint extract to the butter. Place the powdered sugar on top and let it absorb the liquid for about 1 minute. Beat on high speed for about 3 minutes until fully combined.

3. In a cup or small bowl, dissolve the coffee in the hot water and let cool for 2 minutes. Add the coffee mixture and cocoa powder to the bowl and beat for about 2 minutes until combined.

4. Fill a piping bag (no tip required) and fill your macarons. Guide the piping bag about ½ inch above the shells and squeeze a half-dollar–size swirl on top. (The filling will spread.) To stop the filling, flick the piping tip to the side.

5. Refrigerate leftovers, covered, for up to 2 weeks, or freeze for up to 2 months. To reuse, leave at room temperature for a few hours to soften.

ESPRESSO BUTTERCREAM

PREP TIME: 15 minutes

MAKES: 1 cup; enough to fill 12 to 24 macarons

Many people like to wake up with a fresh cup of coffee, but what's the next best thing? A delicious full-bodied espresso buttercream inside an espresso maca-ron. This recipe is easy, using instant coffee instead of freshly brewed. Perfect for the coffee lover in your life!

113 grams (1 stick)
   unsalted butter, at room
   temperature

15 grams (1 tablespoon)
   milk of choice (I prefer
   almond milk)

1 gram (¼ teaspoon)
   vanilla extract

38 grams powdered sugar

2 grams (½ teaspoon)
   instant coffee

1 gram (¼ teaspoon)
   hot water

PERFECT PARTNERS: Use in the Chocolate Macarons (page 30) or Crème Brûlée Macarons (page 96).

1. In a small to medium bowl, with an electric mixer on high speed, beat the butter for about 3 minutes until creamy, white, and fluffy.

2. Add the milk and vanilla to the butter. Place the powdered sugar on top and let it absorb the liquid for about 1 minute. Beat on high speed for about 3 minutes until fully combined.

3. In a cup or small bowl, dissolve the coffee in the hot water and let cool for 2 minutes. Add the coffee mixture to the bowl and beat for about 2 minutes until combined.

4. Fill a piping bag (no tip required) and fill your mac-arons. Guide the piping bag about ½ inch above the shells and squeeze a half-dollar–size swirl on top. (The filling will spread.) To stop the filling, flick the piping tip to the side.

5. Refrigerate leftovers, covered, for up to 2 weeks, or freeze for up to 2 months. To reuse, leave at room temperature for a few hours to soften.

CARROT CAKE BUTTERCREAM

PREP TIME: 15 minutes

MAKES: 1 cup; enough to fill 12 to 24 macarons

If you haven't tried a carrot cake macaron, you're in for an unexpectedly delicious treat! Freeze-dried carrots can be found online, and adding them to the cream cheese buttercream with cinnamon and nutmeg really makes this macaron reminiscent of the classic cake.

85 grams (¾ stick)
   unsalted butter, at room
   temperature

28 grams (2 tablespoons)
   cream cheese, at room
   temperature

1 gram (¼ teaspoon)
   vanilla extract

38 grams powdered sugar

4 grams (1 teaspoon)
   freeze-dried carrot

2 grams (½ teaspoon)
   ground cinnamon

2 grams (½ teaspoon)
   ground nutmeg

PERFECT PARTNERS: Use in the Crunchy Cinnamon Cereal Macarons (page 68) or Toasted Almond Macarons (page 42).

1. In a small to medium bowl, with an electric mixer on high speed, beat the butter and cream cheese for about 3 minutes until creamy, white, and fluffy.

2. Add the vanilla to the butter and cream cheese. Place the powdered sugar on top and let it absorb the liquid for about 1 minute. Beat on high speed for about 3 minutes until fully combined.

3. In a food processor, pulse the freeze-dried carrot into a powder. Add the carrot powder, cinnamon, and nutmeg to the bowl and beat for about 2 minutes until well combined.

4. Fill a piping bag (no tip required) and fill your macarons. Guide the piping bag about ½ inch above the shells and squeeze a half-dollar–size swirl on top. (The filling will spread.) To stop the filling, flick the piping tip to the side.

5. Refrigerate leftovers, covered, for up to 2 weeks, or freeze for up to 2 months. To reuse, leave at room temperature for a few hours to soften.

PUMPKIN PIE/PUMPKIN SPICE LATTE BUTTERCREAM

PREP TIME: 15 minutes

MAKES: 1 cup; enough to fill 12 to 24 macarons

Oh, the fun of autumn, when you go to pumpkin patches, cuddle up and watch scary movies, and drink pumpkin spice lattes. You can make this fall buttercream into a pumpkin spice latte flavor or keep it as classic pumpkin pie.

113 grams (1 stick) unsalted butter, at room temperature

15 grams (1 tablespoon) milk of choice (I prefer almond milk)

1 gram (¼ teaspoon) vanilla extract

38 grams powdered sugar

10 grams canned pumpkin puree

2 grams (½ teaspoon) pumpkin pie spice

2 grams (½ teaspoon) instant coffee (for Pumpkin Spice Latte)

1 gram (¼ teaspoon) hot water (for Pumpkin Spice Latte)

PERFECT PARTNERS: Use in the Crunchy Cinnamon Cereal Macarons (page 68) or Cookie Butter Macarons (page 70).

1. In a small to medium bowl, with an electric mixer on high speed, beat the butter for about 3 minutes until creamy, white, and fluffy.

2. Add the milk and vanilla to the butter. Place the powdered sugar on top and let it absorb the liquid for 1 minute. Beat on high speed for about 3 minutes until fully combined.

3. Add the pumpkin puree and pumpkin pie spice. *For pumpkin spice latte buttercream:* In a small bowl, dissolve the coffee in the hot water, let cool for 2 minutes, and add it to the bowl. Beat for about 2 minutes until combined.

4. Fill a piping bag (no tip required) and fill your macarons. Guide the piping bag about ½ inch above the shells and squeeze a half-dollar–size swirl on top. (The filling will spread.) To stop the filling, flick the piping tip to the side.

5. Refrigerate leftovers, covered, for up to 2 weeks, or freeze for up to 2 months. To reuse, leave at room temperature for a few hours to soften.

RASPBERRY CHEESECAKE BUTTERCREAM

PREP TIME: 15 minutes
MAKES: 1 cup; enough to fill 12 to 24 macarons

Raspberry and cheesecake go well together because they are both tart and sweet! Using freeze-dried raspberries imparts more fruit flavor to the buttercream.

85 grams (¾ stick)
  unsalted butter, at room
  temperature
28 grams (2 tablespoons)
  cream cheese, at room
  temperature
1 gram (¼ teaspoon)
  vanilla extract
38 grams powdered sugar
4 grams (1 teaspoon)
  freeze-dried raspberries

PERFECT PARTNERS: Use in the Lemon Macarons (page 32) or Strawberry Macarons (page 34).

1. In a small to medium bowl, with an electric mixer on high speed, beat the butter and cream cheese for about 3 minutes until creamy, white, and fluffy.

2. Add the vanilla to the butter and cream cheese. Place the powdered sugar on top and let it absorb the liquid for about 1 minute.

3. In a food processor, pulse the freeze-dried raspberries into a powder. Add the raspberry powder to the bowl and beat on high speed for about 3 minutes until fully combined.

4. Fill a piping bag (no tip required) and fill your macarons. Guide the piping bag about ½ inch above the shells and squeeze a half-dollar–size swirl on top. (The filling will spread.) To stop the filling, flick the piping tip to the side.

5. Refrigerate leftovers, covered, for up to 2 weeks, or freeze for up to 2 months. To reuse, leave at room temperature for a few hours to soften.

CRÈME BRÛLÉE CUSTARD BUTTERCREAM

PREP TIME: 15 minutes

COOK TIME: 5 minutes, plus 2 hours to cool

MAKES: 1 cup; enough to fill 12 to 24 macarons

This unique buttercream is rich, decadent, and reminiscent of the popular dessert. It tastes like a custard, with the creamy egg yolks, and pairs perfectly with the torched-sugar macaron shells. It also gives you a use for those leftover egg yolks!

45 grams egg yolks (from about 2 medium eggs)

½ teaspoon vanilla bean paste

40 grams sugar

55 grams whole milk

165 grams unsalted butter, at room temperature

PERFECT PARTNERS: Use in the Pistachio Macarons (page 44) or Red Velvet Macarons (page 54).

1. In a small bowl, whisk the egg yolks, vanilla bean paste, and sugar to combine. Set aside.

2. In a small saucepan over medium-high heat, heat the milk for 3 to 5 minutes until bubbles form around the edge of the pan. While whisking constantly to prevent curdling, pour the milk over the egg yolk mixture. Pour the entire mixture into the saucepan and return it to medium-high heat. Cook, whisking and watching closely, until the mixture reaches 180°F. Pour the custard into a small bowl and refrigerate for about 2 hours until cool.

3. In a small to medium bowl, with an electric mixer on medium-high speed, beat the butter for about 3 minutes until white, fluffy, and smooth.

4. Add the custard and beat for 2 to 3 minutes until combined.

5. Fill a piping bag (no tip required) and fill your macarons. Guide the piping bag about ½ inch above the shells and squeeze a half-dollar–size swirl on top. (The filling will spread.) To stop the filling, flick the piping tip to the side.

6. Refrigerate leftovers, covered, for up to 2 weeks, or freeze for up to 2 months. To reuse, leave at room temperature for a few hours to soften.

PISTACHIO BUTTERCREAM

PREP TIME: 15 minutes

MAKES: 1 cup; enough to fill 12 to 24 macarons

Pistachio macarons can be found in any Parisian pâtisserie and most traditional bakeries. Pistachio's roasted, nutty flavor complements many other flavors and is one of my most popular choices.

113 grams (1 stick) unsalted butter, at room temperature

15 grams (1 tablespoon) milk of choice (I prefer almond milk)

1 gram (¼ teaspoon) vanilla extract

38 grams powdered sugar

25 grams shelled roasted pistachios

PERFECT PARTNERS: Use in the Salted Caramel Macarons (page 60) or Chocolate Macarons (page 30).

1. In a small to medium bowl, with an electric mixer on high speed, beat the butter for about 3 minutes until creamy, white, and fluffy.

2. Add the milk and vanilla to the butter. Place the powdered sugar on top and let it absorb the liquid for about 1 minute. Beat on high speed for about 3 minutes until fully combined.

3. In a food processor, pulse the pistachios until finely chopped. Add the chopped pistachios to the bowl and beat for about 2 minutes until combined.

4. Fill a piping bag (no tip required) and fill your macarons. Guide the piping bag about ½ inch above the shells and squeeze a half-dollar–size swirl on top. (The filling will spread.) To stop the filling, flick the piping tip to the side.

5. Refrigerate leftovers, covered, for up to 2 weeks, or freeze for up to 2 months. To reuse, leave at room temperature for a few hours to soften.

TOASTED ALMOND BUTTERCREAM

PREP TIME: 15 minutes

MAKES: 1 cup; enough to fill 12 to 24 macarons

Although macarons are made of almonds, this buttercream takes the almond flavor to the next level. Using almond butter and almond extract really amps up the flavor. This flavor choice, similar to pistachio buttercream, is a great option for people who don't like overly sweet fillings.

113 grams (1 stick) unsalted butter, at room temperature

15 grams (1 tablespoon) milk of choice (I prefer almond milk)

1 gram (¼ teaspoon) vanilla extract

1 gram (¼ teaspoon) almond extract

38 grams powdered sugar

15 grams almond butter

PERFECT PARTNERS: Use in the Pistachio Macarons (page 44) or Chocolate Macarons (page 30).

1. In a small to medium bowl, with an electric mixer on high speed, beat the butter for about 3 minutes until creamy, white, and fluffy.

2. Add the milk, vanilla, and almond extract to the butter. Place the powdered sugar on top and let it absorb the liquid for about 1 minute. Add the almond butter and beat on high speed for about 3 minutes until fully combined.

3. Fill a piping bag (no tip required) and fill your macarons. Guide the piping bag about ½ inch above the shells and squeeze a half-dollar–size swirl on top. (The filling will spread.) To stop the filling, flick the piping tip to the side.

4. Refrigerate leftovers, covered, for up to 2 weeks, or freeze for up to 2 months. To reuse, leave at room temperature for a few hours to soften.

HAZELNUT CHOCOLATE BUTTERCREAM

PREP TIME: 15 minutes

MAKES: 1 cup; enough to fill 12 to 24 macarons

Hazelnuts and chocolate make a decadent, rich flavor combination that goes nicely in macarons. The creaminess of the chocolate-hazelnut spread mixed with the chopped hazelnuts creates a unique and interesting taste, perfect with any decadently flavored macarons!

113 grams (1 stick)
unsalted butter, at room
temperature

15 grams (1 tablespoon)
milk of choice (I prefer
almond milk)

1 gram (¼ teaspoon)
vanilla extract

38 grams powdered sugar

25 grams hazelnuts, finely
chopped

50 grams chocolate-hazelnut
spread (such as Nutella)

> **PERFECT PARTNERS:** Use in the Espresso Macarons (page 58) or Chocolate Macarons (page 30).

1. In a small to medium bowl, with an electric mixer on high speed, beat the butter for about 3 minutes until creamy, white, and fluffy.

2. Add the milk and vanilla to the butter. Place the powdered sugar on top and let it absorb the liquid for about 1 minute. Beat on high speed for about 3 minutes until fully combined.

3. Add the hazelnuts to the bowl, along with the chocolate-hazelnut spread, and beat for about 2 minutes until combined.

4. Fill a piping bag (no tip required) and fill your macarons. Guide the piping bag about ½ inch above the shells and squeeze a half-dollar–size swirl on top. (The filling will spread.) To stop the filling, flick the piping tip to the side.

5. Refrigerate leftovers, covered, for up to 2 weeks, or freeze for up to 2 months. To reuse, leave at room temperature for a few hours to soften.

WHITE RABBIT CANDY BUTTERCREAM

PREP TIME: 15 minutes

COOK TIME: 20 minutes, plus 15 minutes to cool

MAKES: 1 cup; enough to fill 12 to 24 macarons

White Rabbit candy is a milky, creamy candy from China that can be found at most Asian grocery stores or online. In this recipe, I melt it down into a syrup and pour it into the buttercream. Try this technique with any candy you enjoy!

55 grams heavy
   (whipping) cream
90 grams White
   Rabbit candies
113 grams (1 stick)
   unsalted butter, at room
   temperature
4 grams (1 teaspoon)
   vanilla extract
10 grams powdered sugar

PERFECT PARTNERS:
Use in the Matcha Green Tea Macarons (page 48) or Strawberry Macarons (page 34).

1. In a small saucepan over low heat, combine the heavy cream and candies (you can include the edible rice paper wrappers, if you like). Heat for 15 to 20 minutes, stirring frequently, until the candy is completely melted with no lumps. Put the saucepan in the freezer for 15 minutes, or until the mixture is cooled.

2. In a small to medium bowl, with an electric mixer on high speed, beat the butter for about 3 minutes until creamy, white, and fluffy.

3. Add the cooled candy mixture, vanilla, and powdered sugar to the bowl. Beat on high speed for about 3 minutes until fully combined.

4. Fill a piping bag (no tip required) and fill your macarons. Guide the piping bag about ½ inch above the shells and squeeze a half-dollar–size swirl on top. (The filling will spread.) To stop the filling, flick the piping tip to the side.

5. Refrigerate leftovers, covered, for up to 2 weeks, or freeze for up to 2 months. To reuse, leave at room temperature for a few hours to soften.

TOFFEE FILLING

PREP TIME: 15 minutes

COOK TIME: 15 minutes, plus up to 1 hour to chill

MAKES: 1 cup; enough to fill 12 to 24 macarons

This sticky, chewy toffee filling is good enough to eat on its own! I use store-bought chewy caramel candies, such as Werther's, and melt them into a ganache-like cream. I like to make this around the holidays, but it's delicious any time of year.

198 grams (7 ounces, or ½ can) sweetened condensed milk

70 grams (2.5 ounces) soft caramel candies, unwrapped

30 grams (2 tablespoons) unsalted butter

PERFECT PARTNERS: Use in the Pistachio Macarons (page 44) or Mocha Macarons (page 56).

1. In a small saucepan, stir together the condensed milk, candies, and butter. Place the pan over medium-low heat and bring the mixture to a boil, stirring constantly with a wooden spoon to prevent burning. Once boiling, reduce the heat to low and simmer for 10 to 15 minutes, stirring constantly, until very thick, like fudge. It is ready when you run your spoon through the middle of the toffee and you can see the bottom of the pan before it slowly incorporates again. Refrigerate for 30 minutes to 1 hour to harden, without it turning rock solid.

2. Fill a piping bag (no tip required) and fill your macarons. Guide the piping bag about ½ inch above the shells and squeeze a half-dollar–size swirl on top. (The filling will spread.) To stop the filling, flick the piping tip to the side.

3. Refrigerate leftovers, covered, for up to 2 weeks, or freeze for up to 2 months. To reuse, leave at room temperature for a few hours to soften.

MOCHA GANACHE

PREP TIME: 15 minutes

COOK TIME: 5 minutes, plus 30 minutes to cool

MAKES: 1 cup; enough to fill 12 to 24 macarons

Chocolate and coffee make a perfect pair. The decadence of the chocolate and the bitterness of the coffee make a ganache that's thick, delicious, and rich. This filling goes with many other decadent flavors as well, such as cinnamon, espresso, or hazelnut chocolate.

113 grams heavy
(whipping) cream

113 grams semisweet
chocolate chips

2 grams (½ teaspoon)
instant coffee

PERFECT PARTNERS: Use in the Tiramisu Macarons (page 62) or Chocolate Macarons (page 30).

1. In a small saucepan over medium-high heat, heat the cream for 3 to 5 minutes until bubbles start to form around the edge of the pan. Remove the pan from heat and add the chocolate chips. Let sit for a minute to melt the chocolate. Add the instant coffee and whisk until completely smooth.

2. Scrape the ganache into a heatproof bowl and let cool at room temperature for about 30 minutes until it is a smooth, thick consistency. You can also refrigerate the ganache, checking every few minutes, until it is smooth and thick, but not hard.

3. Fill a piping bag (no tip required) and fill your macarons. Guide the piping bag about ½ inch above the shells and squeeze a half-dollar–size swirl on top. (The filling will spread.) To stop the filling, flick the piping tip to the side.

4. Refrigerate leftovers, covered, for up to 2 weeks, or freeze for up to 2 months. To reuse, leave at room temperature for a few hours to soften.

CHOCOLATE MINT GANACHE

PREP TIME: 15 minutes
COOK TIME: 5 minutes, plus 30 minutes to cool
MAKES: 1 cup; enough to fill 12 to 24 macarons

Fresh mint and chocolate are a match made in heaven—refreshing and delicious. This ganache is reminiscent of mint chocolate chip ice cream, and it's perfect for summertime!

113 grams heavy
 (whipping) cream
113 grams semisweet
 chocolate chips
1 gram (¼ teaspoon)
 peppermint extract

PERFECT PARTNERS: Use in the Hazelnut Chocolate Macarons (page 100) or Strawberry Macarons (page 34).

1. In a small saucepan over medium-high heat, heat the cream for 3 to 5 minutes until bubbles start to form around the edge of the pan. Remove the pan from heat and add the chocolate chips. Let sit for a minute to melt the chocolate. Add the peppermint extract and whisk until completely smooth.

2. Scrape the ganache into a heatproof bowl and let cool at room temperature for about 30 minutes until it has a smooth, thick consistency. You can also refrigerate the ganache, checking every few minutes, until it is smooth and thick, but not hard.

3. Fill a piping bag (no tip required) and fill your macarons. Guide the piping bag about ½ inch above the shells and squeeze a half-dollar–size swirl on top. (The filling will spread.) To stop the filling, flick the piping tip to the side.

4. Refrigerate leftovers, covered, for up to 2 weeks, or freeze for up to 2 months. To reuse, leave at room temperature for a few hours to soften.

TEA WHIPPED WHITE CHOCOLATE GANACHE

PREP TIME: 15 minutes

COOK TIME: 10 minutes, plus 1 to 2 hours to chill

MAKES: 1 cup; enough to fill 12 to 24 macarons

This whipped white chocolate ganache is versatile—it can be infused with almost anything, including any type of tea. I like to whip it so it has the texture of a buttercream. Be careful in hot weather, as the ganache may melt.

113 grams white chocolate callets (see page 12)

28 grams (2 tablespoons) unsalted butter, diced, at room temperature

80 grams heavy (whipping) cream

5 grams (1 tablespoon) loose tea leaves (dark-roast oolong, Earl Grey, jasmine, or Thai)

Pinch kosher salt

PERFECT PARTNERS: Use in the Pistachio Macarons (page 44) or Matcha Green Tea Macarons (page 48).

1. In a small to medium heatproof bowl, combine the white chocolate and butter. Set aside.

2. In a small saucepan over medium heat, use a wooden spoon to stir together the heavy cream and tea leaves. Cook for 5 to 10 minutes, stirring, until the mixture bubbles around the edges and the tea has steeped into the cream, turning it brown.

3. Pour the hot cream through a fine mesh strainer into the bowl with the chocolate and butter and let sit for a minute, then stir until completely smooth. Stir in the salt. Freeze for 1 hour, or refrigerate for 2 hours.

4. When ready to use, with an electric mixer on medium speed, whip the cold ganache for about 3 minutes until light and fluffy.

5. Fill a piping bag (no tip required) and fill your macarons. Guide the piping bag about ½ inch above the shells and squeeze a half-dollar–size swirl on top. (The filling will spread.) To stop the filling, flick the piping tip to the side.

6. Refrigerate leftovers, covered, for up to 2 weeks, or freeze for up to 2 months. To reuse, leave at room temperature for a few hours to soften.

HONEY LAVENDER WHIPPED WHITE CHOCOLATE GANACHE

PREP TIME: 15 minutes

COOK TIME: 10 minutes, plus 1 to 2 hours to chill

MAKES: 1 cup; enough to fill 12 to 24 macarons

Honey and lavender is a sophisticated flavor combination that's for not everyone, but it is a classic in France, and perfect for floral dessert lovers.

113 grams white chocolate callets (see page 12)

28 grams (2 tablespoons) unsalted butter, diced, at room temperature

80 grams heavy (whipping) cream

4 grams (1 tablespoon) culinary-grade lavender

21 grams (1 tablespoon) honey

Pinch kosher salt

PERFECT PARTNERS: Use in the Lemon Macarons (page 32) or Vanilla Macarons (page 28).

1. In a small to medium heatproof bowl, combine the white chocolate and butter. Set aside.

2. In a small to medium saucepan over medium heat, use a wooden spoon to stir together the heavy cream and lavender. Cook for 5 to 10 minutes, stirring, until the mixture bubbles around the edges and the tea has steeped into the cream.

3. Pour the hot cream through a fine-mesh strainer into the bowl with the chocolate and butter and let sit for a minute, then stir until completely smooth.

4. Stir in the honey and then the salt. Freeze for 1 hour, or refrigerate for 2 hours.

5. When ready to use, with an electric mixer on medium speed, whip the cold ganache for about 3 minutes until light and fluffy.

6. Fill a piping bag (no tip required) and fill your macarons. Guide the piping bag about ½ inch above the shells and squeeze a half-dollar–size swirl on top. (The filling will spread.) To stop the filling, flick the piping tip to the side.

7. Refrigerate leftovers, covered, for up to 2 weeks, or freeze for up to 2 months. To reuse, leave at room temperature for a few hours to soften.

WHITE CHOCOLATE GANACHE
(WITH WHITE CHOCOLATE RASPBERRY VARIATION)

PREP TIME: 15 minutes

COOK TIME: 5 minutes, plus 30 minutes to cool

MAKES: 1 cup; enough to fill 12 to 24 macarons

This white chocolate ganache can be flavored many ways. This version has less cream than the whipped versions (see pages 195 and 196), making it a bit sweeter and thicker. Raspberries balance the sweetness. This ganache goes well with macadamia nuts, as in the White Chocolate Macadamia Macarons (page 102).

65 grams heavy
(whipping) cream

113 grams white chocolate
callets (see page 12)

4 grams (1 teaspoon)
freeze-dried raspberries
(for the raspberry version)

PERFECT PARTNERS:
Use in the Matcha Green
Tea Macarons (page 48)
or Tiramisu Macarons
(page 62).

1. In a small saucepan over medium-high heat, heat the cream for 3 to 5 minutes until bubbles start to form around the edge of the pan. Remove the pan from the heat and add the white chocolate. Let sit for a minute to melt the chocolate.

2. *For the raspberry ganache*: In a food processor, pulse the freeze-dried raspberries into a powder, then add the powder to the ganache and whisk until completely smooth.

3. Scrape the ganache into a heatproof bowl and let cool at room temperature for 30 minutes until it is a smooth, thick consistency. You can also refrigerate the ganache, checking every few minutes, until it is smooth and thick, but not hard.

4. Fill a piping bag (no tip required) and fill your macarons. Guide the piping bag about ½ inch above the shells and squeeze a half-dollar–size swirl on top. (The filling will spread.) To stop the filling, flick the piping tip to the side.

5. Refrigerate leftovers, covered, for up to 2 weeks, or freeze for up to 2 months. To reuse, leave at room temperature for a few hours to soften.

Heart Macarons page 122

Measurement Conversions

VOLUME EQUIVALENTS	U.S. STANDARD	U.S. STANDARD (OUNCES)	METRIC (APPROXIMATE)
LIQUID	2 tablespoons	1 fl. oz.	30 mL
	¼ cup	2 fl. oz.	60 mL
	½ cup	4 fl. oz.	120 mL
	1 cup	8 fl. oz.	240 mL
	1½ cups	12 fl. oz.	355 mL
	2 cups or 1 pint	16 fl. oz.	475 mL
	4 cups or 1 quart	32 fl. oz.	1 L
	1 gallon	128 fl. oz.	4 L
DRY	⅛ teaspoon		0.5 mL
	¼ teaspoon		1 mL
	½ teaspoon		2 mL
	¾ teaspoon		4 mL
	1 teaspoon		5 mL
	1 tablespoon		15 mL
	¼ cup		59 mL
	⅓ cup		79 mL
	½ cup		118 mL
	⅔ cup		156 mL
	¾ cup		177 mL
	1 cup		235 mL
	2 cups or 1 pint		475 mL
	3 cups		700 mL
	4 cups or 1 quart		1 L
	½ gallon		2 L
	1 gallon		4 L

OVEN TEMPERATURES

FAHRENHEIT	CELSIUS (APPROXIMATE)
250°F	120°C
300°F	150°C
325°F	165°C
350°F	180°C
375°F	190°C
400°F	200°C
425°F	220°C
450°F	230°C

WEIGHT EQUIVALENTS

U.S. STANDARD	METRIC (APPROXIMATE)
½ ounce	15 g
1 ounce	30 g
2 ounces	60 g
4 ounces	115 g
8 ounces	225 g
12 ounces	340 g
16 ounces or 1 pound	455 g

Resources

Amazon.com
Almond flour, baking equipment, baking extracts, baking pans, edible gold/silver paint, food colorings, macaron baking mats, mixing bowls, piping bags, packaging

AmeriColor.com
Gel food colorings

BakingCalculators.com
Easy baking measurement converter

BedBathandBeyond.com
Baking equipment, kitchen torches

Gygi.com
Baking supplies, packaging, white chocolate

LoveandMacarons.blogspot.com (Natalie's blog)
Find templates for characters, designs, shapes, and other macaron tips on my blog

Nuts.com
Almond flour, baking extracts, and nuts (fast shipping)

OliveNation.com
Unique flavored baking extracts, chocolate, white chocolate

SurlaTable.com
Baking equipment, macaron baking mats

TheSugarArt.com
Edible gold, powdered super pigmented food coloring, etc.

YouTube.com/user/nataliewongg
My macaron baking tutorial, and other macaron baking tips

Index

A

Aging egg whites, 9–10
Almond flour, 3, 7
Almonds
    Toasted Almond
        Buttercream, 189
    Toasted Almond
        Macarons, 42–43
    Vegan Toasted Almond
        Macarons, 156–157

B

Baking mats, silicone, 5–6
Banana Macarons,
    Chocolate, 98–99
Berries
    Blueberry Matcha Latte
        Macarons, 82–83
    Nut-Free/Vegan Strawberry
        Buttercream, 160
    Raspberry Cheesecake
        Buttercream, 186
    Raspberry Cheesecake
        Macarons, 90–91
    Raspberry Macarons, 36–37
    Strawberry Buttercream, 166
    Strawberry Macarons, 34–35
    Strawberry Shortcake
        Macarons, 92–93
    White Chocolate Ganache
        (with White Chocolate
        Raspberry variation), 197
Birthday Cake Macarons, 108–109
Black Sesame Buttercream, 181
Black Sesame Macarons, 74–75
Blueberry Matcha Latte
    Macarons, 82–83

Blue with Gold Splatter
    Macarons, 112–113
Bunny Macarons, 128–129
Butter, 12

C

Candy
    White Rabbit Candy
        Buttercream, 191
    White Rabbit Candy
        Macarons, 104–105
Cane sugar, 8
Caramel
    Salted Caramel
        Buttercream, 178
    Salted Caramel Macarons, 60–61
    Toffee Filling, 192
Carrot Cake Buttercream, 184
Carrot Cake Macarons, 94–95
Cereal
    Crunchy Cinnamon Cereal
        Macarons, 68–69
    Fruity Cereal Buttercream, 172
    Fruity Cereal Macarons, 66–67
Chickpeas, 11
Chocolate, 12
    Chocolate Banana
        Macarons, 98–99
    Chocolate Buttercream, 165
    Chocolate Macarons, 30–31
    Chocolate Mint Ganache, 194
    Chocolate Mint
        Macarons, 40–41
    Cookies and Cream
        Buttercream, 175
    Cookies and Cream
        Macarons, 72–73

Hazelnut Chocolate
    Buttercream, 190
Hazelnut Chocolate
    Macarons, 100–101
Mocha Ganache, 193
Mocha Macarons, 56–57
Nut-Free Chocolate
    Macarons, 144–145
Nut-Free/Vegan Chocolate
    Ganache, 159
Peppermint Mocha
    Buttercream, 182
Polar Bear Peppermint Mocha
    Macarons, 134–135
Red Velvet Macarons, 54–55
Tiramisu Macarons, 62–63
Turkey-Shaped
    Hazelnut Chocolate
    Macarons, 132–133
Vegan Chocolate
    Macarons, 152–153
Christmas. *See also* Winter
    Reindeer Toffee
        Macarons, 130–131
Cinnamon
    Cinnamon Buttercream, 173
    Crunchy Cinnamon Cereal
        Macarons, 68–69
Coconut
    Pandan Coconut
        Buttercream, 171
    Pandan Coconut
        Macarons, 84–85
    Pineapple Coconut
        Buttercream, 170
    Pineapple Coconut
        Macarons, 86–87

Coffee
    Espresso Buttercream, 183
    Espresso Macarons, 58–59
    Mocha Ganache, 193
    Mocha Macarons, 56–57
    Nut-Free Espresso
        Macarons, 146–147
    Nut-Free/Vegan Espresso
        Buttercream, 161
    Peppermint Mocha
        Buttercream, 182
    Polar Bear Peppermint Mocha
        Macarons, 134–135
    Tiramisu Macarons, 62–63
Confectioners' sugar, 8
Cookie Butter Buttercream, 174
Cookie Butter Macarons, 70–71
Cookies and Cream
    Buttercream, 175
Cookies and Cream
    Macarons, 72–73
Cream cheese
    Carrot Cake Buttercream, 184
    Cream Cheese Buttercream, 176
    Raspberry Cheesecake
        Buttercream, 186
    Crème Brûlée Custard
        Buttercream, 187
Crème Brûlée Macarons, 96–97

D

Dehumidifiers, 2, 6

E

Earl Grey Macarons, 46–47
Easter
    Bunny Macarons, 128–129
    Easter Egg Macarons, 120–121
Eggnog
    Eggnog Buttercream, 177
    Snowman Eggnog
        Macarons, 126–127
Egg sizes, 10

Egg whites, 8–10
Equipment, 2, 3–7
Extracts, 10

F

Fans, electric, 6
Fillings
    Black Sesame Buttercream, 181
    Carrot Cake Buttercream, 184
    Chocolate Buttercream, 165
    Chocolate Mint Ganache, 194
    Cinnamon Buttercream, 173
    Cookie Butter Buttercream, 174
    Cookies and Cream
        Buttercream, 175
    Cream Cheese Buttercream, 176
    Crème Brûlée Custard
        Buttercream, 187
    Eggnog Buttercream, 177
    Espresso Buttercream, 183
    Fruity Cereal Buttercream, 172
    Hazelnut Chocolate
        Buttercream, 190
    Honey Lavender Whipped White
        Chocolate Ganache, 196
    Lemon Buttercream, 167
    Mango Buttercream, 168
    Matcha Buttercream, 179
    Mocha Ganache, 193
    Nut-Free/Vegan Chocolate
        Ganache, 159
    Nut-Free/Vegan Espresso
        Buttercream, 161
    Nut-Free/Vegan Strawberry
        Buttercream, 160
    Nut-Free/Vegan Vanilla
        Buttercream, 158
    Pandan Coconut
        Buttercream, 171
    Passion Fruit Guava
        Buttercream, 169
    Peppermint Mocha
        Buttercream, 182

    Pineapple Coconut
        Buttercream, 170
    Pistachio Buttercream, 188
    Pumpkin Pie/Pumpkin Spice
        Latte Buttercream, 185
    Raspberry Cheesecake
        Buttercream, 186
    Rose Buttercream, 180
    Salted Caramel Buttercream, 178
    step-by-step guide, 16–17
    Strawberry Buttercream, 166
    Tea Whipped White Chocolate
        Ganache, 195
    Toasted Almond
        Buttercream, 189
    Toffee Filling, 192
    Vanilla Buttercream, 164
    White Chocolate Ganache
        (with White Chocolate
        Raspberry variation), 197
    White Rabbit Candy
        Buttercream, 191
Flavorings, 10
Food colorings, 10–11, 23
    Blue with Gold Splatter
        Macarons, 112–113
    Galaxy Macarons, 116–117
    Pink with Gold Brush
        Macarons, 114–115
    Rainbow Swirl Macarons, 118–119
French meringue, 13
Fruits, freeze-dried, 12

G

Galaxy Macarons, 116–117
Ghost Pumpkin Spice Latte
    Macarons, 124–125
Gold dust
    Blue with Gold Splatter
        Macarons, 112–113
    Pink with Gold Brush
        Macarons, 114–115
Granulated sugar, 8

Guava
    Passion Fruit Guava
        Buttercream, 169
    Passion Fruit Guava
        Macarons, 88–89

H

Half-sheet pans, 6
Halloween
    Ghost Pumpkin Spice Latte
        Macarons, 124–125
Hazelnuts
    Hazelnut Chocolate
        Buttercream, 190
    Hazelnut Chocolate
        Macarons, 100–101
    Turkey-Shaped
        Hazelnut Chocolate
        Macarons, 132–133
Heart Macarons, 122–123
Honey Lavender Macarons, 50–51
Honey Lavender Whipped
    White Chocolate
    Ganache, 196
Humidity, 2

I

Ingredients
    basics, 7–10
    measuring, 2, 3–4
    nut-free, 11
    vegan, 11

J

Jasmine Milk Tea
    Macarons, 80–81

L

Lavender
    Honey Lavender
        Macarons, 50–51
    Honey Lavender Whipped White
        Chocolate Ganache, 196

Lemon Buttercream, 167
Lemon Macarons, 32–33

M

Macadamia Macarons, White
    Chocolate, 102–103
Macaronage, 14
Macarons
    advanced skills, 23–24
    step-by-step guide, 12–17
    troubleshooting, 18–22
Mango Buttercream, 168
Mango Macarons, 38–39
Matcha
    Blueberry Matcha Latte
        Macarons, 82–83
    Matcha Buttercream, 179
    Matcha Green Tea
        Macarons, 48–49
    Nut-Free Matcha
        Green Tea
        Macarons, 148–149
Mint
    Chocolate Mint Ganache, 194
    Chocolate Mint
        Macarons, 40–41
    Peppermint Mocha
        Buttercream, 182
    Polar Bear Peppermint Mocha
        Macarons, 134–135
    Vegan Mint Macarons, 154–155
Mixers, 4–5
Mixing bowls, 4
Mocha Ganache, 193
Mocha Macarons, 56–57

N

Nut-free
    ingredients, 11
    Nut-Free Chocolate
        Macarons, 144–145
    Nut-Free Espresso
        Macarons, 146–147

Nut-Free Matcha Green Tea
    Macarons, 148–149
Nut-Free Vanilla
    Macarons, 142–143
Nut-Free/Vegan Chocolate
    Ganache, 159
Nut-Free/Vegan Espresso
    Buttercream, 161
Nut-Free/Vegan Strawberry
    Buttercream, 160
Nut-Free/Vegan Vanilla
    Buttercream, 158
Nuts
    Hazelnut Chocolate
        Buttercream, 190
    Hazelnut Chocolate
        Macarons, 100–101
    Pistachio Buttercream, 188
    Pistachio Macarons, 44–45
    Toasted Almond
        Buttercream, 189
    Toasted Almond
        Macarons, 42–43
    Vegan Toasted Almond
        Macarons, 156–157
    White Chocolate Macadamia
        Macarons, 102–103

O

Oat flour, 11
Oolong Tea Macarons,
    Dark-Roast, 76–77
Oven thermometers, 6

P

Pandan Coconut
    Buttercream, 171
Pandan Coconut Macarons, 84–85
Passion Fruit Guava
    Buttercream, 169
Passion Fruit Guava
    Macarons, 88–89
Pastry bags and tips, 5

Peppermint Mocha
Buttercream, 182
Pineapple Coconut
Buttercream, 170
Pineapple Coconut
Macarons, 86–87
Pink with Gold Brush
Macarons, 114–115
Piping batter, 14–15
Pistachio Buttercream, 188
Pistachio Macarons, 44–45
Polar Bear Peppermint Mocha
Macarons, 134–135
Powdered sugar, 8
Pumpkin pie spice
Ghost Pumpkin Spice Latte
Macarons, 124–125
Pumpkin Pie Macarons, 110–111
Pumpkin Pie/Pumpkin Spice
Latte Buttercream, 185

R

Rainbow Swirl Macarons, 118–119
Raspberries
Raspberry Cheesecake
Buttercream, 186
Raspberry Cheesecake
Macarons, 90–91
Raspberry Macarons, 36–37
White Chocolate Ganache
(with White Chocolate
Raspberry variation), 197
Recipes, about, 24–25
Red Velvet Macarons, 54–55
Reindeer Toffee
Macarons, 130–131
Resting batter, 15
Rose Buttercream, 180
Rose Macarons, 52–53

S

Salt, 8
Salted Caramel Buttercream, 178

Salted Caramel
Macarons, 60–61
Scales, digital, 3–4
Separating egg whites, 9
Shortcake Macarons,
Strawberry, 92–93
Sifters, 6
Snowman Eggnog
Macarons, 126–127
Spatulas, 5
Storage, 17
Strawberries
Nut-Free/Vegan
Strawberry
Buttercream, 160
Strawberry Buttercream, 166
Strawberry Macarons, 34–35
Strawberry Shortcake
Macarons, 92–93
Sugars, 8
Sunflower seed flour, 11

T

Tea
Blueberry Matcha Latte
Macarons, 82–83
Dark-Roast Oolong Tea
Macarons, 76–77
Earl Grey Macarons, 46–47
Jasmine Milk Tea
Macarons, 80–81
Matcha Buttercream, 179
Matcha Green Tea
Macarons, 48–49
Nut-Free Matcha
Green Tea
Macarons, 148–149
Tea Whipped White
Chocolate
Ganache, 195
Thai Tea Macarons, 78–79
Temperature, baking, 3, 6
Thai Tea Macarons, 78–79

Thanksgiving
Pumpkin Pie Macarons, 110–111
Turkey-Shaped
Hazelnut Chocolate
Macarons, 132–133
Tiramisu Macarons, 62–63
Toffee
Reindeer Toffee Macarons,
130–131
Toffee Filling, 192
Troubleshooting, 18–22
Turkey-Shaped Hazelnut
Chocolate Macarons,
132–133
Tuxedo Macarons, 136–137

V

Valentine's Day
Heart Macarons, 122–123
Vanilla
Nut-Free Vanilla
Macarons, 142–143
Nut-Free/Vegan Vanilla
Buttercream, 158
Vanilla Buttercream, 164
Vanilla Macarons, 28–29
Vegan Vanilla Macarons, 150–151
Vegan
ingredients, 11
Nut-Free/Vegan Chocolate
Ganache, 159
Nut-Free/Vegan Espresso
Buttercream, 161
Nut-Free/Vegan Strawberry
Buttercream, 160
Nut-Free/Vegan Vanilla
Buttercream, 158
Vegan Chocolate
Macarons, 152–153
Vegan Mint Macarons, 154–155
Vegan Toasted Almond
Macarons, 156–157
Vegan Vanilla Macarons, 150–151

W

Weddings
  Tuxedo Macarons, 136–137
  Wedding Dress
    Macarons, 138–139
Weighing ingredients, 2, 3–4, 9
White chocolate, 12
  Honey Lavender Whipped White
    Chocolate Ganache, 196

Tea Whipped White Chocolate
    Ganache, 195
White Chocolate
    Ganache (with White
    Chocolate Raspberry
    variation), 197
White Chocolate Macadamia
    Macarons, 102–103
White Rabbit Candy
    Buttercream, 191

White Rabbit Candy
    Macarons, 104–105
Winter
  Polar Bear Peppermint Mocha
    Macarons, 134–135
  Reindeer Toffee
    Macarons, 130–131
  Snowman Eggnog
    Macarons, 126–127

ACKNOWLEDGMENTS

It's so exciting to be able to write a second book. I am truly grateful to Callisto Media for giving me another amazing opportunity to expand off my last book. I want to thank Salmon Taymuree for scouting me and guiding me through the process. I appreciate all the support. I want to thank Anna Pulley for being such a great, kind, and understanding editor. Thank you to the rest of the Callisto Media team for being on this project with me. I really love to share my macaron knowledge with others, and I'm glad I could do it again. I also want to thank all my amazing customers and Instagram supporters; this wouldn't be possible without you. I would also like to shout out to my property owner and property management team for my bakery; thank you for the amazing opportunities as well. Next, I want to thank my friends and family for helping me with my business—it enabled me to write this book while baking orders for people around the Bay Area. Lastly, thank you to all the readers who read my last book, *Macarons for Beginners*, which is now the number one best seller in macarons on Amazon.

ABOUT THE AUTHOR

Natalie Wong is a Bay Area native who has loved to bake ever since she was a little girl. She found her true calling in 2013 when she started her own macaron business, and wrote a blog called *Love and Macarons*, which racked up more than 100,000 views across the world. She quit her full-time job in commercial real estate in 2019 to pursue her passion for baking macarons. In the same year, she also wrote her first book, published with Callisto Media, *Macarons for Beginners*, which is now proudly the number one best seller for macarons on Amazon. She recently opened her own bakery: Yours Truly Bakery Café in Castro Valley, California. In her spare time, she enjoys hanging out with her boyfriend and friends, taking care of her new house, walking her dog, Bebe, at the park, and cooking delicious meals. You can follow her on Instagram @MacaronsByNatalie and @AlwaysYours.CV, or check out her website MacaronsByNatalie.com. She also has a few instructional videos on her YouTube channel (YouTube.com/user/nataliewongg). Email Natalie at: nataliemacarons@gmail.com.

CPSIA information can be obtained
at www.ICGtesting.com
Printed in the USA
JSHW050230110222
22668JS00001BA/1